A WORKSHOP ON

The Book of Mark

A Dramatic Account of the Life of Jesus

CAROLYN NYSTROM

Lamplighter Books Grand Rapids, Michigan
Zondervan Publishing House

A Workshop on the Book of Mark
A Dramatic Account of the Life of Jesus
Copyright © 1987 by Carolyn Nystrom
All rights reserved

Previously published as *Who Is Jesus?/ A Woman's Workshop on Mark*

Lamplighter Books are published by the Zondervan Publishing House
1415 Lake Drive, S.E., Grand Rapids, Michigan 49506

ISBN 0-310-42001-6

Edited by Pamela M. Hartung

Printed in the United States of America

90 91 92 93 94 / LP / 6 5 4 3 2

CONTENTS

MARK'S STORY OF JESUS

If you are looking for a dull book to help you go to sleep, don't try the Book of Mark. Mark's gospel opens when Jesus starts His public ministry, and it plunges into a breathtaking series of miracles, teaching, and argument, then ends when He is seen alive again after having been killed. Throughout the book, Jesus is shown as a servant to both God and man, even though His power reveals Him to be no less than God the Son.

Who wrote this lively account of Jesus' life? Its author was a young man named John Mark, a cousin of Barnabas, who was Paul's early missionary partner. While still young, John Mark was active in the early church and, for reasons not entirely explained, was the source of a disagreement between Paul and Barnabas—a disagreement serious enough to split that missionary team.[1] Barnabas went his way with

---

[1] Acts 15:37–39.

Mark, while Paul continued his work with a new partner, Silas. Later Mark and Paul were reconciled, and Mark was with Paul when Paul wrote some of the letters that fill major portions of the New Testament. When Paul was near death, he asked that Mark be sent to be with him.[2]

Mark was probably a teenager during Christ's lifetime. Perhaps he clung near the fringes of the crowd that followed Jesus. He may have been the young man who, collared by a soldier during Jesus' arrest, wriggled out of his robe and dashed naked into the darkness to escape.[3] But when Mark started to write his book, he needed more than these distant observations. He needed inside information. It was probably aggressive Peter, Jesus' companion and disciple throughout His ministry, who gave Mark most of the data for his book. Like Peter, Mark's account is one of action couched in strong, blunt words. You can almost see the brawny fisherman sitting by a campfire telling John Mark what he had seen and heard.

The Book of Mark is the shortest of the four gospels, but it records more miracles than any of the others. Christ's ceaseless activity among needy people continues without stopping as He willingly chooses to go to Jerusalem and certain execution. The last third of the book tells of this final week in Christ's life.

Mark ends with a mystery. The oldest records stop abruptly at Mark 16:8—right in the middle of a thought, as if an ancient scroll had been torn and the last piece lost. What else did Mark have to say? We can only guess. But we do have fifteen and a half chapters of rapid-fire narrative, so take a deep breath and get ready for action. Here comes Mark's story of Jesus.

---

[2] 2 Timothy 4:11.
[3] Mark 14:51—52.

I'VE JOINED THE GROUP. NOW WHAT?

You've joined a group of people who agree that the Bible is worth studying. For some it is the Word of God and therefore a standard for day-to-day decision. Others may say the Bible is merely a collection of interesting teachings and tales, worthy of time and interest but not much more. You may place yourself at one end of this spectrum or the other. Or you may fit somewhere in between. But you have one goal in common with other people in your group: to enjoy studying the Bible together.

A few simple guidelines will not only help you meet this goal but also prevent needless problems.

1. Take a Bible with you. Any modern translation is fine. Suggested versions include: *Revised Standard Version, New American Standard Bible, Today's English Version, New International Version, Jerusalem Bible, New American Bible,* and *New English Bible.*

A few versions, however, do not work well in group Bible

study. For beautiful language the *King James Version* is unsurpassed. Yours may bear great sentimental value because it belonged to your grandmother. But if you use a *King James Version*, you will spend a great deal of effort translating the Elizabethan English into today's phrasing, perhaps losing valuable meaning in the process.

Paraphrases like *Living Bible, Phillips,* and *Amplified* are especially helpful in private devotions, but they lack the accuracy of a translation by Bible scholars. Therefore leave these at home on Bible study day.

If you would like to match the phrasing of the questions in this guide, use the *New International Version.* If, however, you fear that any Bible is far too difficult for you to understand, try *Today's English Version.* This easy-to-read translation is certain to change your mind.

2. Arrive at Bible study on time. You'll feel as if you are half a step behind throughout the entire session if you miss the Bible readings and opening survey questions.

3. Call your host or hostess if you are going to be absent. This saves him or her from setting a place for you if refreshments are served. It also frees the group to begin on time without waiting needlessly for you.

When you miss a session, study the passage independently. The gospel of Mark forms a story. You'll feel more able to participate when you return if you have studied the intervening material.

4. Volunteer to be a host or hostess. A quick way to feel as if you belong is to have the Bible study meet in your home.

5. Decide if you are a talker or a listener. This is a discussion Bible study, and for a discussion to work well, all persons should participate more or less equally. If you are a talker, count to ten before you speak. Try waiting until several others speak before you give your own point of view.

If you are a listener, remind yourself that just as you benefit from what others say, they profit from your ideas. Besides, your insights will mean more even to you if you put them into words and say them out loud. So take courage and speak.

6. Keep on track. This is a group responsibility. Remember that you are studying the Book of Mark. Although a speech, magazine article, or some other book may be related, discussion of it will take time away from the main object of your study. In the process the whole group may go off on an interesting but time-consuming tangent, making the leader's job more difficult.

While the Bible is consistent within itself and many excellent topical studies build on its consistency, the purpose of this study is to examine Mark's story of Jesus. Therefore making cross-references (comparing a passage with other portions of Scripture) will cause the same problems as any other tangent. In addition to confusing the people who are unfamiliar with other parts of the Bible, making cross-references may cause you to miss Mark's intent in the passage before you.

Naturally once you have studied a section of Mark as a group, you may refer to it. Mark assumed his readers would have the earlier passages in mind as they read each new section.

7. Help pace the study. Each study should last about an hour and fifteen minutes. With the questions and your Bible in front of you, you can be aware of whether the study is progressing at an adequate pace. Each group member shares the responsibility of seeing that the entire passage is covered and that the study is brought to a profitable close.

8. Don't criticize another church or religion. You might find that the quiet person across the table attends that church—and he won't be back to your group.

9. Get to know people in your group. Call each other

during the week, between meetings. Meet socially; share a car pool when convenient; offer to take in a meal if another group member is ill. You may discover that you have more in common than a willingness to study the Bible. Perhaps you'll add to your list of friends.

10. Get ready to lead. It doesn't take a mature Bible student to lead this study. Just asking the questions in this guide should prompt a thorough digging into the passage. Besides, you'll find a hefty section of leader's notes in the back in case you feel a little insecure. So once you've attended the group a few times, sign up to lead a discussion. Remember, the leader learns more than anyone else.

ME, A LEADER?

Sure. Many Bible study groups share the responsibility of leading the discussion. Sooner or later your turn will come. Here are a few pointers to quell any rising panic and help you keep the group working together toward its common goal.

1. Prepare well ahead of time. Preparing a week or two in advance is not too much. Read the Scripture passage every day for several successive days. Go over the questions, writing out possible answers in your book. Check the leader's helps at the back of the book for additional ideas, then read the questions again—several times—until the sequence and wording seem natural to you. Don't let yourself be caught during the study with that "now I wonder what comes next" feeling. Take careful note of the major areas of application. Try living them for a week. By then you will discover some of the difficulties others in your group will face when they try to do the same. Finally, pray. Ask God to lead you as you lead the group. Ask Him to make you sensitive to people, to the Scripture, and to Himself. Expect to grow. You will.

2. Pace the study. Begin on time. People have come for the purpose of studying the Bible. You don't need to apologize for that. At the appointed time simply announce that it is time to begin, open with prayer, and launch into the study.

Keep an eye on the clock throughout the study. These questions are geared to last for about an hour and fifteen minutes. Don't spend forty-five minutes on the first three questions and then find you have to rush through the rest. On the other hand if the questions are moving by too quickly, the group is probably not discussing each one thoroughly enough. Slow down. Encourage people to interact with each other's ideas. Be sure they are working through all aspects of the questions.

Then end—*on time*. Many people have other obligations immediately after the study and will appreciate a predictable closing time.

3. Read the passage aloud by paragraphs—not verses. Verse-by-verse reading causes a brief pause after each verse and breaks the flow of the narrative; this makes it harder to understand the total picture.

4. Ask, don't tell. This study guide is designed for a discussion moderated by a leader. It is not a teacher's guide. When you lead the group, your job is like that of a traffic director. You gauge the flow of discussion, being careful that everyone gets a turn. You decide which topics will be treated and in what order. You call a halt now and then to send traffic in a new direction. But you do not mount a soapbox and lecture.

Your job is to help each person in the group personally discover the meaning of the passage and share that discovery with the others. Naturally, since you have prepared the lesson in advance, you will be tempted to tell them all you've learned. Resist this temptation until others have had a chance to discover the same things. Then, if something is still missing, you may add your own insights to the collection.

5. Avoid tangents. The bane of any discussion group is that oh-so-interesting lure of a tangent. These are always time consuming and rarely as profitable as the planned study. A few red flags will warn you that a tangent is about to arise. They are, "My pastor says . . ."; "I read that . . ."; "The other day Suzie . . ."; "If we look at Ezekiel (or John or Revelation) . . ."

If this occurs, politely listen to the first few sentences. If they confirm your suspicion that a tangent is indeed brewing, thank the person, then kindly but firmly direct attention back to the passage.

A leader does, however, need to be sensitive to pressing needs within the group. On rare occasions the tangent grows out of a need much more important than any preplanned study. In these cases whisper a quick prayer for guidance and follow the tangent.

6. Talk about application. Each study in this guide leads to a discussion that applies the point of the passage to real life. If you are short of time or if your group feels hesitant about discussing personal things, you'll entertain the thought of omitting these questions. But if you do, your group will lose the main purpose of the study. If God's Word is a book to live by, a few people in your group ought to be willing to talk about how they are going to live in response to it. Putting these intentions into words will strengthen their ability to live out the teachings. The listeners will be challenged to do the same. So always pace the study so that you allow adequate time to talk over the application questions. Be prepared also to share from your own experience of trying to live out the passage.

7. Try a prayer and share time. Many groups start their sessions with fifteen minutes of coffee, then hold a short time of sharing personal concerns, needs, and answers to prayer. Afterward the group members pray briefly for each other, giving thanks and praise and asking together that God will meet the needs expressed. These short, informal sentence prayers are much like casual conversation. The group members simply turn their conversation away from each other and toward God. For many this brief time of prayer becomes a weekly lifeline.

8. Enjoy leading. It's a big responsibility but a rewarding one.

BIBLE STUDY SCHEDULE

Date	Passage	Leader	Host or Hostess
	Mark 1		
	Mark 2		
	Mark 3		
	Mark 4:1–34		
	Mark 4:35–5:43		
	Mark 6		
	Mark 7		
	Mark 8		
	Mark 9:1–32		
	Mark 9:33–10:16		
	Mark 10:17–52		
	Mark 11:1–12:12		
	Mark 12:13–44		
	Mark 13		
	Mark 14		
	Mark 15:1–16:8		

Names and Phone Numbers

—Please Call Host or Hostess If You Cannot Attend—

Tyre

Caesarea Philippi

SYRIA

Mediterranean Sea

GALILEE

Bethsaida

Capernaum

Cana

Sea of Galilee

Gennesaret

Gergesa

Nazareth

Gadara

Caesarea

SAMARIA

Jordan River

Samaria

DECAPOLIS

Sychar

Mt. Gerizim

PEREA

Joppa

Jericho

Jerusalem

Bethphage

Bethany

Bethlehem

JUDEA

Dead Sea

IDUMEA

Beersheba

PALESTINE IN THE TIME OF JESUS

1

HERE COMES JESUS!

Mark 1

I once dreamed about Jesus. It wasn't a vision, nothing supernatural at all, just an ordinary dream with the characters and actions merging together in typical surrealistic dream-like quality and only half-remembered in the morning.

What startled me into remembering the dream was that Jesus looked so different from any artist's painting. Artists seem to make Jesus stand still with an attitude of great wisdom, as if posing for a portrait on a breezeless day. But the Jesus of my dream was young, strong, virile, and literally galloping across sandy Judean trails. He stopped for a moment to smile, touch, heal, and then was gone, robes hiked high and dust puffs scattering at his heels.

The writer Mark could well have sketched my dream. Through his eyes I can see children playing with sticks in the dust, an excited shout, "Here comes Jesus!" a quick vignette of His face close to theirs. But if I don't look fast, He's gone— on to another scene and another work.

Read aloud all of Mark 1.

1. If this chapter were your introduction to Jesus, what would be your first impressions? _____

_____

_____

2. Notice the title of the book in verse 1. What would you expect to find in a book with this title? _____

_____

_____

3. a. List all the place names in this chapter and locate them on the map on page 16. _____

_____

_____

b. List all the phrases that refer to time. (You should find at least a dozen.) _____

_____

_____

_____

_____

c. What do these tell you about the way Jesus went about His work? _____

_____

Look again at verses 1–20.

4. In what different ways did John prepare the way for Jesus? _____

_____

_____

_____

5. What can you know about the relationship between the three members of the Trinity from its appearance here?

_____

_____

6. Notice Christ's first recorded sermon in verse 15. What could His hearers know from this message? _____

_____

_____

7. Why do you think Jesus called these two sets of brothers to follow Him? _____

_____

_____

8. a. What indication do you see that Jesus was beginning to get a broad hearing? _____

_____

_____

b. What problems did this larger audience create?

_____

9. The people in the synagogue at Capernaum were amazed at Christ's authority. Survey the rest of the chapter and list the different areas in which you see Jesus exercising that authority. _____

_____

_____

_____

10. What indicates that Jesus balanced His work of teaching with His work of healing? _____

_____

_____

11. a. Evil spirits, or demons, appear throughout the Book of Mark. What can you know of these beings from what you see here? _____

_____

_____

_____

b. What connection can you see between Christ's temptation in the desert and His later encounter with demons? _____

_____

_____

12. a. Why do you think Jesus took time in the early morning darkness to be alone with His Father? _____

_____

b. When has a time of prayer alone with God been of special significance to you? _____

_____

_____

c. How do you arrange your routine to provide for these times of prayer? _____

_____

_____

d. If you decided to follow Christ's example by spending time alone praying to God, how could you rearrange your schedule to do this? _____

_____

_____

13. In what different ways did Jesus show love and understanding toward people? (Use the whole chapter.)

_____

_____

_____

_____

14. a. If you had walked through this chapter with Jesus and heard Him say, "Follow me," would you have followed Him? _____

b. What all would you consider before making that choice? _____

_____

_____

2

IS JESUS GOD?

Mark 2

"Oh, I believe that Jesus was God all right," said the woman across the Bible study table, "He just didn't know it." My eyes opened wide. In many years of small group Bible studies I've heard my share of off-the-wall interpretations of Scripture. But this was a new one. That particular thought had never occurred to me. I filed it in the back recesses of my brain. Later I'd make a mental run-through of the Gospels. If my friend's idea were wrong, I'd find evidence to refute it there.

As we might expect from a person as direct as the writer of Mark, he wastes no time addressing such an important issue. It is true that Jesus did not go around pounding His chest and shouting, "I am God." He seemed instead to prefer that people discover His true nature gradually, through His teaching and works, and through their own response to Him—as if gradual absorption made more lasting faith. But

22

the evidence, if we look for it, is present. As you study, let Jesus reveal Himself to you.

Read aloud Mark 2:1–12.

1. Assume the role of one character in this scene. Now tell the story through his or her eyes. Use the information in the text, but feel free to add your own embellishments. *Characters:*

One of the four friends

The paralyzed man

The owner of the house

A teacher of the law

A member of the crowd

2. a. What was the center of controversy here between Jesus and the teachers of the law? _____

_____

_____

b. What reasons did these teachers have to take Jesus seriously? _____

_____

_____

_____

Read aloud Mark 2:13–17.

3. a. What would be the disadvantages to Jesus of having Levi as a disciple? _____

_____

b. In view of these, why do you think Jesus invited Levi to follow Him? _____

_____

_____

4. Why was it easier for Levi to follow Jesus than for the teachers of the law to follow Him? _____

_____

_____

5. What does this illustration of Levi as a new disciple suggest about the way a person must come to Christ?

_____

_____

Read aloud Mark 2:18–22.

6. Explain in your own words Christ's metaphor of the wedding. Who do the characters represent? What are the events? _____

_____

_____

_____

7. What could the Pharisees have understood about Christ from the metaphor of old wineskins and new wine?

_____

_____

_____

8. a. In what way is following Christ like "new wine" to you? _____

_____

b. When have you seen incompatibility between this "new wine" and the "old wineskins" of life without Christ?

_____

_____

Read aloud Mark 2:23–28.

9. How did Jesus try to bridge the Sabbath controversy with the Pharisees? _____

_____

_____

10. If "the Sabbath is made for man," but Jesus is Lord of the Sabbath, how can you reflect both of these truths in your own observance of Sabbath? (What should you do and not do? What should you teach your children about Sabbath?)

_____

_____

_____

11. In summary, find one question from the Jewish religious leaders in each of the four paragraphs you discussed. Explain in your own words Christ's answer to each question. _____

_____

_____

_____

_____

_____

_____

12. How did each of these controversies help define Christ's nature? (Try giving a name to Jesus based on each paragraph.) _____

_____

_____

_____

13. Suppose a person following Jesus through the events in this chapter had wondered, "Is Jesus God?" What information here would help that person answer the question? _____

_____

_____

14. a. Each encounter with Jesus in this chapter provoked a change. What is Jesus changing in your life? _____

_____

_____

b. What would you like Him to change in you?

_____

_____

_____

3

WHO IS CHRIST'S FAMILY?

Mark 3

"I'm glad you didn't move to Colorado," said Craig, our youngest. I thought back to our plans some fifteen years ago. We'd been all set to leave the boring plains of Illinois and spend the rest of our lives with mountain ranges in the background. But a teaching job had fallen through at the last minute, so we had stayed put.

I'd almost forgotten those frustrating days. And I'd even learned to enjoy the birds and prairie flowers of the plains. Now my ten-year-old son brought it back.

"Why, Craig? Why are you glad we didn't move to Colorado?"

"'Cause then you wouldn't have been here to adopt me."

We hugged. "I'm glad God kept us here too, so we could adopt you," I said, though I hadn't actually thought of it that way before.

Families are special to God. So when Jesus began to speak

of the most important relationship a person can have with God, He used the language of the family—an adopted family.

Read aloud all of Mark 3.

　1. What made it hard for Jesus to do His work? _____

_____

_____

Look more carefully at verses 1–6.

　2. a. If Jesus had wanted to keep peace with the Pharisees, how might He have handled this scene differently?

_____

_____

　b. Why didn't the Pharisees answer Christ's question (v. 4)? _____

_____

_____

Note: The Herodians were a Jewish party that favored Herod's rule. They were natural enemies of the Pharisees.

　3. In what ways did Christ's actions here illustrate His teaching of Mark 2:27–28? _____

_____

_____

　4. a. Use your map on page 16 to find the places mentioned in verse 8. What does this tell you about the effects of Christ's ministry? _____

_____

_____

b. What practical steps did Jesus take to cope with such large groups of people (vv. 7–19)? _____

_____

_____

5. Why do you think Jesus would not let the evil spirits speak about Him? _____

_____

_____

6. a. What steps led to becoming one of the Twelve?

_____

b. What did Jesus expect of them? _____

_____

7. How should a twentieth-century follower of Jesus carry out some of these same functions? _____

_____

_____

Read again Mark 3:20–35.

8. How did Christ's family's explanation of His behavior differ from the explanation of the teachers of the law?

_____

_____

9. What did Jesus mean by His parables of the kingdom, the house, and the strong man? _____

_____

_____

10. Using the information here, how would you define the eternal sin (v. 29)? _____

_____

_____

11. Why didn't Jesus go home with His family?

_____

_____

12. Even though His words seemed harsh, in what sense was Jesus being kind both to the teachers of the law and to His family? _____

_____

_____

13. Look again at verses 13–15 and verses 34–35. What responsibilities come with a close relationship to Jesus?

_____

_____

14. a. What would (or do) you enjoy about that relationship? _____

_____

_____

b. If you were determined to become a better member of Christ's family, what would be your next step?

_____

_____

4

WHAT HAPPENS WHEN PEOPLE HEAR ABOUT JESUS?

Mark 4:1–34

Is a vegetable garden worth the hassle? It's a question I ask myself every spring as I look out my kitchen window at the 20' by 100' plot of plowed ground my neighbors call a miniature field. I think of long days in the office followed by swatting mosquitoes at dusk as I grub for weeds. I think of spraying for potato bugs, dusting for cabbage worms, and fishing the ones I miss out of the cooking pot. I think of digging out one hundred more rocks that froze and thawed themselves to the surface over the winter. So I look at the grass seed in the hardware store and think, *Why not just have a bigger lawn?* (My husband does the mowing.)

But every spring finds me on my hands and knees sifting wonderfully loose soil through my fingers, feeling the first warm sun in six months on my back. And row by measured row, I plant—beans, peas, corn, broccoli, potatoes, pumpkins, squash, cantaloupe, tomatoes; sunflowers on one end, strawberries on the other, and a border of petunias to perfume the air at twilight. I am a sower. And for all of the hardship that follows, the sowing itself is a joy.

When Jesus began to teach in parables, He talked about gardens and seed and a sower. It was a language His hearers would understand.

Read aloud Mark 4:1–34.

1. Repetition sometimes gives a clue to what is important. What words and phrases are repeated in this passage?

_____

_____

Focus on verses 1–25.

2. A parable places two things side by side for comparison. In this parable, who or what is the sower, the seed, and the soil? _____

_____

_____

3. a. What can you know about the seed in this parable?

_____

_____

b. What can you know about the sower? _____

_____

_____

4. a. Think of the crowds who followed Jesus. Describe the kind of person He must have had in mind for each of the four types of soil. _____

_____

_____

_____

b. What kind of people from your own experience would match those four descriptions? (Think of specific people, but give no names please.) _____

_____

_____

_____

5. a. What kind of soil are you becoming? _____

_____

b. How do you know? _____.

_____

6. Why did Jesus speak in parables? _____

_____

_____

7. Does this parable encourage you or discourage you from sharing Jesus with people who don't know Him? Why?

_____

_____

8. Because Jesus used the parable of the sower to teach His disciples how to understand parables, it is often called "The Parable of Parables." What could Christ's disciples apply to other parables from His teachings about the sower?

_____

_____

_____

Read again Mark 4:21–34.

9. a. What do the "stand" and the used "measure" symbolize? _____

_____

b. What promise and what warning is couched in this parable? _____

_____

_____

10. What new qualities about seeds do these parables describe? _____

_____

_____

11. What can you know about the kingdom of God from these qualities? _____

_____

_____

12. If you were thinking about becoming a follower of Jesus, what effects would the parables you studied today have on that decision? _____

_____

_____

13. If you wanted to use the knowledge God has given you about Himself as "seed," what should you do with it?

_____

_____

5

ARE MY NEEDS TOO BIG FOR JESUS?

Mark 4:35–5:43

"Come to Jesus and all your troubles will end." It's a ploy used by less than careful evangelists in an attempt to bring the reluctant into the fold. Only later do hearers discover that they still have to live by a stiff budget to avoid bankruptcy, see a counselor to preserve their marriage, undergo chemotherapy to treat cancer, or go out and find a job to replace the one they lost.

Did Jesus fail them? By no means. When Jesus walked this earth, He sometimes intervened in nature's course. A wind, a legion of demons, illness, death. He grabbed them by the neck, and they did His bidding: miracles. Rarely today do we see such intervention. But we have that memory written in Scripture. And we serve the same Jesus who has the same power.

Does Jesus make all our troubles end? Not exactly. But He walks us through them, offering His own self-discipline as we stick with a budget, breathing life (perhaps through a counselor) into a dead marriage, healing by chemistry the cells of human bodies He created, and granting the self-confidence (because Jesus loves me) to keep looking in spite of job loss.

We should not expect our walk with Jesus to be free of trouble. But neither should we underrate His power.

1. How do you feel during a storm? _____
What do you like and dislike about a storm? _____

_____

_____

_____

Read aloud Mark 4:35—41.

2. What indications lead you to think that Jesus was exhausted? _____

_____

_____

3. a. Why would experienced sea fishermen wake their spiritual teacher during a storm? _____

_____

_____

b. Why do you think the disciples were afraid *after* the storm ended? _____

_____

_____

_____

Read aloud Mark 5:1–20.

4. a. What words and phrases show the severity of this man's problem? _____

_____

_____

b. What changes reflected healing in this man?

_____

_____

_____

5. a. Who killed the pigs? _____

_____

b. What might Jesus have been intending to teach by allowing the pigs to be destroyed? _____

_____

_____

_____

6. In what different ways do you see Satan at work throughout the events here? _____

_____

_____

_____

_____

7. Why were the people afraid *after* the man was healed?

_____

_____

8. a. What did the people lose by asking Jesus to leave?

_____

_____

   b. Why wouldn't Jesus take the healed man with Him?

_____

_____

Read aloud Mark 5:21–43.

   9. a. What reasons did Jesus have for attending to the problems of Jairus first?

_____

_____

_____

   b. In view of these reasons, why do you think Jesus attended to the woman first? _____

_____

_____

   10. a. Read Leviticus 15:25–28. Jesus stopped everything and publicly declared that this woman had touched Him. Why would that be hard for her? _____

_____

_____

   b. Why would it also be valuable? _____

_____

_____

_____

11. What do you think was going through the mind of Jairus as he watched Jesus with the woman? _____

_____

_____

12. In what ways did Jesus show consideration for the needs of this girl and her family? _____

_____

_____

_____

13. Look back through all of today's reading. Create a title for Jesus based on each of the four miracles. _____

_____

_____

_____

_____

14. Jesus dealt with four different sets of needs in today's Scripture. Bring to mind one of your own current needs. How does this passage encourage you to believe that Jesus can help you with that need? _____

_____

_____

_____

6

WHEN IS BELIEF NOT BELIEF?

Mark 6

I have sat through hundreds of prayer meetings in my life. Many of them have been times of spiritual nurture and family love. My favorite kind of prayer service is one that meets in a living room or around a kitchen table, with only a dozen or fewer people present. In those settings I can sometimes almost physically feel the hugs of prayer as we lift one another to our all-powerful God. Some of my best friendships have grown out of these prayer meetings.

Yet I see a consistent pattern of smallness in the way we pray. Yes, we know we should praise God and thank Him. And the most casual look inside ourselves will show a need for confession. A closer look will spot areas of struggle where we know God is seeking to grow us more like Himself. We see that one part of us tries to grow, while another part holds out white-knuckled resistance.

But what do we pray about? I come away from almost

every prayer meeting with a grocery list of needs. George needs a job. Sara's Aunt Suzie is having a gall-bladder surgery. Bob's kid Ryan is not doing well in school. Chico hasn't heard yet about his college scholarship application. Janet's parents are breaking up.

What does this say about our belief in who Jesus is? Are we any different from Christ's disciples who felt quite comfortable hearing Jesus teach but were astounded that He could create food? Or from the sick and lame of Gennesaret, who pressed Jesus so hard for healing that they left no time to hear Him teach? Do we believe mostly in a Jesus who meets needs?

Belief takes many forms. But a growing, vibrant, mature faith in Christ covers a lot more territory than a grocery list.

Read aloud all of Mark 6.

1. a. What suggests that large numbers of people were hearing about Jesus? _____

_____

_____

_____

_____

b. What problems in His ministry did this create?

_____

_____

_____

_____

_____

Look again at verses 1–6a.

2. What do the questions of verses 1–3 imply about this crowd's perspective of Jesus? _____

_____

_____

3. Why might it have been hard for Jesus to visit Nazareth, His hometown? _____

_____

_____

Look again at verses 6b–13.

4. a. What work did Christ's disciples do on this trip?

_____

b. As you study Christ's words to them, explain how these instructions would help the disciples accomplish this work. _____

_____

_____

_____

_____

5. If this trip were in some sense a training mission, what could the disciples have learned from the experience?

_____

_____

_____

_____

_____

Look again at verses 14–29.

6. Why was Herod concerned about Christ's identity?

_____

_____

7. What different influences did the people here have on Herod? (Consider John, Herodias, her daughter, the guests, and Jesus.) _____

_____

_____

_____

_____

8. What can you know of Herod's character from this account? _____

_____

9. Herod was king over Galilee, where Jesus was doing most of His work. What concerns would have hovered in your mind if you had been helping to carry out Christ's ministry under this kind of king? (Remember Mark 3:6.)

_____

_____

Look again at verses 30–44.

10. How did the events of this day differ from what Jesus had set out to do? _____

_____

_____

11. In what different ways did Jesus show His care for the people who followed Him? _____

_____

_____

12. What could the people who witnessed this miracle have learned from it? _____

_____

_____

_____

Look again at verses 45–56.

13. What reasons did the disciples have to be terrified?

_____

_____

14. In view of verses 51–52, what connection can you see between the miracle of the loaves and the miracle of walking on water? _____

_____

_____

_____

15. Review each of the events recorded in Mark 6. What did people believe about Jesus, and what were the limitations of their faith?

vv. 1–6a _____

_____

vv. 6b–13 _____

_____

vv. 14–29 _____

_____

vv. 30–44 _____

_____

vv. 45–52 _____

_____

vv. 53–56 _____

_____

16. What handicaps do you see in a relationship that is built primarily on what Jesus can do *for* us rather than on what He can do *in* us and *through* us? _____

_____

_____

_____

17. What steps can you take to help your own relationship to Jesus become more complete? _____

_____

_____

_____

7

AM I AS CLEAN AS I THINK I AM?

Mark 7

Raising two small boys is a good way to find out about dirt. In summer they can collect so much of the stuff in the crevices of their suntanned little bodies that I literally have to sweep out the bathtub before I can use it myself. And that doesn't count the dirt they leave on the kitchen floor and the living room carpet on their way to the bathroom.

Small boys will teach you about other kinds of dirt too. I once spent several days driving our first-grader to and from school because he was serving a bus suspension for writing nasty words on the bus windows. (He could barely write his name!) But for that kind of dirt we can look inside ourselves and see much the same thing. Years later the same little boy asked, "Mom, if you were all by yourself and you banged yourself real hard, what would you say?" I thought a long time before I answered that one.

Dirt is all around us. And religious people in Christ's era

worried a lot about touching things or people that made them unclean: a dead body, a sick person, a pig, a sinner. For Christ all that surface clutter was insignificant. He looked inside a person. And what He saw was even more serious.

Read aloud Mark 7:1–23.

1. Describe the issue that raised conflict between Jesus and the religious leaders from Jerusalem. _____

_____

_____

Note: This is the second time representatives have traveled from Jerusalem to visit Jesus. Remember Mark 3:22?

2. Jesus talked about being "unclean" to three groups of people in this passage. Who were they? Which verses did He address to each? What differences do you see in His tone?

_____

_____

_____

3. a. How did the practice of Corban violate the fifth commandment to honor parents? _____

_____

_____

_____

b. Why did Jesus call the religious leaders hypocrites?

_____

4. a. Why did the crowd feel mystified by Christ's description of "unclean"? _____

_____

_____

b. How does Christ's explanation to His disciples clarify His concept of impurity? _____

_____

_____

c. In view of this, why was it useless for the Pharisees to try to wash away their impurity with water? _____

_____

5. What differences do you see between contemporary ethics and Christ's view of what makes a person unclean?

_____

_____

6. a. If you were raising a teenager who, like most teens, valued greatly the way he or she looked, what would you want to teach your child from this passage? _____

_____

_____

b. How could you put into practice Christ's teachings here as you relate to your own parents? _____

_____

_____

7. Look again at the question of verse 5, "Why don't your disciples live according to the tradition . . . ?" In view of the rest of the passage, how would you answer that question?

_____

_____

Read aloud Mark 7:24–30.

8. Was Jesus rude to this woman? Explain. Clue: The word "dogs" here means small household pets. _____

_____

_____

9. In what ways did the woman show faith? _____

_____

_____

10. What did Jesus demonstrate with this miracle? _____

_____

_____

Read aloud Mark 7:31–37.

11. a. What is hard about communicating with a deaf-mute person? _____

_____

_____

b. How do Christ's actions with this man seem particularly appropriate? _____

_____

_____

_____

12. Look back at Mark 5:17–20. What do you think has been going on in this region of Decapolis since Jesus was last there? _____

_____

13. On the map on page 16, trace Christ's movements throughout this chapter. (Begin at Gennesaret in Mark 6:53.) What connection can you see between these travels and Christ's words of verse 19, "Jesus declared all foods 'clean' "? _____

_____

_____

14. a. Read again the list of thirteen sins in verses 21–22. Which of these are frequent sins of even "good" people?

_____

_____

b. What different views of human nature do you see in this description and the Pharisees' view of impurity? _____

_____

_____

15. When you see yourself in the description of verses 21–22, what does Christ's love mean to you? _____

_____

_____

8

WHAT DOES IT COST TO FOLLOW JESUS?

Mark 8

"One dollar and ninety-nine cents," read the sign over the grocery-store salad bar. (Or so I thought.) What a good idea! A busy Saturday seems to always find me trudging up and down the basket-riddled aisles of our neighborhood grocery store. Why I'm always there at noon, my cart piled high with a week's worth of food for six, at the store's busiest time of the week, I couldn't say. My schedule just works out that way.

Today no one was home but my husband. Lunch for two, ready made, for four dollars didn't sound bad at all. I grabbed two plastic trays with hinged lids and piled them high. We'd even have leftovers for supper.

A twenty-minute wait in the checkout line, however, revealed the real truth. Hadn't I read the small print? Those lunches were one dollar and ninety-nine cents *per pound*. I closed my eyes. Reluctantly I shelled out the money.

In much the same way, a moment of reckoning comes in the Book of Mark—a point where one of Christ's disciples recognizes, for sure, who Jesus is. Once this happens, Jesus begins to speak plainly about cost: cost to Him, cost to us who follow Him.

Read aloud all of Mark 8.

1. If you had been one of Christ's disciples during this second mass feeding, what thoughts and questions would be going through your mind? _____

_____

_____

_____

_____

2. What similarities and differences do you see between the mass feeding in Mark 6:30–44 and the miraculous feeding in 8:1–10. (Consider numbers, place, situation that prompted the miracle, and teaching that followed it.)

_____

_____

_____

_____

_____

3. a. Why did the Pharisees want a sign? _____

_____

_____

b. Why do you think Jesus wouldn't give them one?

_____

_____

Look again at verses 14–26.

4. a. Describe the Pharisees as you have seen them thus far in Mark. _____

_____

_____

b. In what ways might the "yeast" of the Pharisees infect the disciples? _____

_____

_____

_____

_____

5. How did Jesus demonstrate sensitivity to the needs of the blind man? _____

_____

_____

_____

6. In what sense did the healing of the blind man demonstrate what it was like to have "eyes but fail to see"?

_____

_____

7. What would be the symptoms of this kind of half-sight in our spiritual vision? _____

_____

_____

8. a. Under what circumstances have you felt that you had eyes and ears for Jesus but somehow failed to see and hear?

_____

_____

_____

b. How would you want other believers to pray for you in a time like that? _____

_____

_____

Look again at verses 27–38.

9. How would the different ideas about Christ's identity affect the way people responded to Him? _____

_____

_____

_____

Note: Peter's statement of verse 29 forms a watershed division in the Book of Mark. From this point on Jesus devotes most of His energy to teaching His disciples and preparing them for His death. Only three miracles remain.

10. Why should Peter's statement initiate such a change in Christ's ministry? _____

_____

_____

_____

11. What did Jesus say would happen to Him? to His followers? _____

_____

_____

12. Was Jesus unkind to Peter? Explain. _____

_____

_____

Look again at verses 34—38.

13. If you were thinking of following Jesus, what questions would these verses encourage you to ask? _____

_____

_____

14. What reasons do you find here to follow Jesus?

_____

_____

15. a. If you have already become a follower of Jesus, what has it cost you? _____

_____

_____

b. What do you consider its rewards? _____

_____

_____

9

CAN JESUS HELP MY UNBELIEF?

Mark 9:1–32

The most valuable person in my Bible study group is an unbeliever. I came to that realization one day as I mentally reviewed where one of my groups had been—and where it was headed. Sue (not her real name) was a person who latched onto every pious platitude that dared cross the lips of some careless Christian and said, "I don't believe that; it's garbage and here's why." Whereupon she would explain at length any real or imagined logical fallacy in the statement, while the careless speaker sputtered and squirmed.

Uncomfortable? Yes. But Sue made people think. She bared the unbelief of people in her group, unbelief that they often covered with sugary statements about love and trust. And oddly, once that unbelief was laid open, genuine faith began to take root—a carefully examined faith that dared to stand against the wind.

As for Sue, God hasn't left her out. Could her unbelief, vociferously expressed, become a first step toward faith?

Read aloud Mark 9:1–13.

1. In what different ways do you see the power and glory of Jesus displayed here? _____

_____

_____

2. What could the appearance of Moses and Elijah with Jesus symbolize to these three disciples? _____

_____

_____

3. What was wrong with Peter's idea? _____

_____

_____

4. a. Look again at the conversation that took place on the way down the mountain. What seems to be the disciples' major concern? _____

_____

_____

b. What was Christ's main concern? _____

_____

_____

5. Read Malachi 4:5–6, the last words of the Old Testament. Read also Matthew 17:11–13. In view of these passages, what value would it be to the disciples to see Elijah with Jesus at this time? _____

_____

_____

6. How would Christ's allusion here to Elijah address the hope that Jesus would set up a strong political kingdom?

_____

_____

_____

7. Read again verse 7. When has a "mountain-top experience" increased your ability to listen to Jesus?

_____

_____

Read aloud Mark 9:14–32.

8. What pressures were the remaining nine disciples facing? _____

_____

_____

9. Recall the previous accounts of demon possession in the Book of Mark. In what ways is this occurrence similar? How is it different? _____

_____

_____

_____

_____

_____

10. What do you admire in the boy's father? _____

_____

_____

_____

11. List the many different ways you see unbelief at work throughout this passage. _____

_____

_____

_____

12. When is spiritual unbelief healthy? _____

_____

_____

13. How could the experiences of this passage help unbelief progress into faith? _____

_____

_____

14. When has God used your own unbelief as a step toward faith? _____

_____

_____

15. What do you need Jesus to help you believe right now? _____

_____

_____

10

WHAT MAKES A STRONG FAMILY?

Mark 9:33–10:16

What made the family I grew up in strong? God knows it had weaknesses, and I know them too. I even spent time in my early adult years mentally counting out those weaknesses, partly so I could avoid them in my own home. My success was limited. I avoided their mistakes but made an equal number of my own. Only as I began to raise my own children did I more fully appreciate the strengths my mother and father had built into our family network.

I grew up the oldest of five in a crumbling tenant farmhouse in southwestern Ohio. We were poor; our house wouldn't let us deny that. But my father worked every day. His factory job was low paying, but he kept at it—a perseverance I see in myself. And he raised the most beautiful flowers for miles around. Though our house looked like a strong wind would topple it, people often slowed their cars to admire the lovely yard. I doubt they even noticed the house.

And my mother treated each child as a special gift. She didn't drive, and we didn't have money for extra activities anyway, so our life was mostly spent at home. You'd think she'd be glad to get rid of us on the rare occasions we were away. Not true. Her welcome-home hugs said she'd missed us and was really glad to see us again.

And my parents stuck with each other: through illness and economic loss and challenges of faith. We kids used to play a silly game with my mother. "Which one do you love best?" we asked. Her answer? "I love your daddy best." Somehow that answer made us feel secure. We knew there was no chance that we could manipulate our way between Mom and Dad. They simply put each other first—ahead of self, ahead of us.

Now as I study Scripture, I realize how many of God's principles for family strength were ingredients in my own growing-up years. I hope my own children can say the same.

1. What was the greatest strength of the family in which you grew up? _____

_____

_____

Read aloud Mark 9:33–37.

2. How did Christ's two illustrations point out error in the disciples' values? _____

_____

_____

3. a. What's hard about being a servant? _____

_____

b. Think of your most significant relationship with people. If you were to become a Christlike servant in that relationship, what changes would you have to make?

_____

4. According to this passage, why is a child important?

_____

_____

5. a. What attitudes and actions say "welcome" to a child? _____

_____

_____

b. How could you make your own children feel more welcome in your home? If you do not have children, how could you better express "welcome" to the children you know? _____

_____

_____

_____

Read aloud Mark 9:38–41.

6. How could this teaching help people who do Christ's work to respect each other? _____

_____

_____

_____

7. How should verse 41 affect your attitude toward receiving help from other believers? _____

_____

_____

Read aloud Mark 9:42–50.

8. Biblical writers sometimes use hyperbole (deliberate exaggeration) to emphasize truth. What does Jesus want His hearers to think and feel as they read these words?

_____

_____

_____

9. In view of verse 42, what steps could you take to teach your children the serious nature of sin and still preserve their sense of self-worth? _____

_____

_____

10. How does the disciples' argument (vv. 33–34) conflict with their call to be "salt" in the world (v. 50)? _____

_____

_____

Read aloud Mark 10:1–12.

11. a. What is the difference between Moses' command about divorce and Christ's teaching? _____

_____

_____

b. What reasons does Jesus give for that difference?

_____

_____

Note: The Bible gives two acceptable reasons for divorce. Jesus permitted divorce if one partner had been sexually unfaithful (Matt. 5:31–32). Paul permitted divorce if a Christian had been deserted by an unbelieving spouse (1 Cor. 7:10–16).

We should notice that even in these hard circumstances, God *allows* divorce; He never demands it. Many Christian marriages have survived and even have grown through the determined love of one partner, even in the face of such severe damage.

12. If a couple were to take seriously, from the beginning of their relationship, the teachings here, how would it affect their dating, courtship, and marriage? _____

_____

_____

_____

_____

_____

Read aloud Mark 10:13–16.

13. Contrast the disciples' behavior with the teachings of Mark 9:35–37, 42. Compare how they seem to value children with how Jesus values children. _____

_____

_____

_____

_____

_____

14. What do you think Jesus had in mind when He told the disciples to receive the kingdom of God "like a child"?

_____

_____

15. In what different ways did Jesus show His concern for children? (Use the whole passage.) _____

_____

_____

_____

_____

_____

16. Review each of the five sections you studied. Find one principle in each that, if you followed it, would improve your own family relationships. _____

_____

_____

_____

_____

17. Think of one person in your family whose relationship with you could use some repair work. What practical step, based on the teachings of this passage, could you take this week to begin that repair? _____

_____

_____

11

WILL JESUS TURN ME INTO A SERVANT?

Mark 10:17–52

One of the hardest lessons I've had to learn as a wife and mother is to be a servant. The truth is I'd much rather be a leader and leave the serving to someone else. The muddy boot tracks jubilantly skipped across my kitchen floor symbolize a hundred other slights: dinner two hours in preparation gobbled down (with only mild complaints) in ten minutes, vacation designed for toddlers (or teens) but not for adults, an evening hovered over fifth-grade fractions for the fourth kid in line. (So much for a night of fun and fellowship with friends from church.) Add to that scrubbing toilets, fishing dirty underwear from under beds, sponging up vomit, and arriving at church well-dressed but as soggy as the leaky diaper on the baby I cradled in my lap. No wonder it's easy for mothers to feel that all of life consists of putting something into bodies or mopping up what oozes out of them.

Yet the wife/mother job description also calls me to be a

leader. I must give wise counsel to my teens about dating, sex, and marriage—and I must lay the groundwork well ahead of time. I must exert firm authority as I break up a stone-throwing match among the twenty grade-school kids who wait for the school bus in my driveway. I must speak persuasively to the school-board curriculum committee as I outline a course of high-school study that gives equal advantages to both honors and vocational students.

Servant-leader, leader-servant. Jesus calls me to be both. The manner in which I lead in each situation will be colored by the fact that I am also a servant: a servant to my family, a servant to my church, a servant to my community, a servant to God. Just in case I get confused juggling those apparently opposite roles, Jesus Himself led the way.

Read aloud Mark 10:17–31.

1. What do you admire in this rich man? _____

_____

_____

2. What reasons did the disciples have to be amazed at Christ's teachings? _____

_____

_____

3. Could you do what Jesus asked this man to do? Would it be easier or harder if you were more wealthy than you are now? Why? _____

_____

_____

_____

4. What hope and caution does Jesus offer those who want eternal life? _____

_____

_____

Read aloud Mark 10:32–34.

5. a. On the map on page 16, trace Christ's recent journey. (Begin at Mount Hermon in Mark 9:3.) See also Mark 9:30; 9:33; and 10:1.

b. What motives might the disciples have imagined in Jesus as they joined Him in this steady journey southward?

_____

_____

6. If they believed what Jesus said, what could His disciples now know about His immediate future? (Review also 8:31–32; 9:12–13; and 9:31–32.) _____

_____

_____

_____

Read aloud Mark 10:35–45.

7. What reasons did the ten disciples have for feeling indignant toward James and John? _____

_____

_____

8. How does Christ's teaching about service reply both to the request of James and John and to the indignant remaining ten? _____

_____

_____

9. Look again at the words of verse 43, "Not so with you." What would you expect to see in a Christian leader who was this kind of servant? _____

_____

_____

10. Bible scholars speak of verse 45 as the key verse to all of Mark, perhaps even a key to the entire New Testament. What do you know about Jesus that would give this statement such merit? _____

_____

_____

Read aloud Mark 10:46–52.

11. a. What obstacles did Bartimaeus have to overcome in order to receive his sight? _____

_____

_____

b. How did Christ's actions with Bartimaeus demonstrate His teachings in the previous paragraph?_____

_____

_____

12. Review Christ's teaching about the relative position of people (Mark 9:33–37; 10:13–16; 10:31; 10:42–45). What tensions do you see between these teachings and the way the rest of the world values people? _____

_____

_____

_____

_____

13. If you were to live out Christ's teachings here, how would you behave differently from most of your neighbors?

_____

_____

Bartimaeus

He began to cry out, "Jesus, Son of David.
Have mercy on me!" And many were sternly
telling him to be quiet (Mark 10:47–48).

The man's been sitting here, begging
for half a century, listening to the coins clink,
fingerpicking the imprint of Caesar,
but never witnessing the high buy
of gold in the art market.

The man's been thinking, trying
to stitch together his childhood fabric
of remembered color: trying to clasp
and take to eye the drub of brown,
and the fleet felt of yellow, the hum of gold,
and the glaze of blue; but they're all
fused to a grim gray in the burned-out
electrodes of the optic nerve.
It's like looking for a drip of green
in a Pollock panorama.

The man's been fretting over?
The man's been giving up every day
since the morning the sun failed to rise
in his retina; and when he hears the tramp
of mob feet, learns the name of the Son
poised at the tip, finds out it's the blind man's
never bluff, always enough, makes-them-see-surety,
and he starts shouting—bonkers, riproaring,

absolutely determined "Hear me! Hear me!"
New Year's Eve—Fourth of July hurrah
    noise-making—
for this is the thing he's dreamed about,
wept about, screamed in his deepest heart for
    months about—

And these toads are telling him
to tie his tongue?[1]

---

[1] Mark R. Littleton, *The Other Side* (January, 1984). Used by permission.

12

WHO GIVES JESUS AUTHORITY?

Mark 11:1–12:12

I don't like authority—unless, of course, it's my own. I spent most of my teen years feeling quite certain that I would never marry because I doubted I'd ever find anyone I could submit to and thereby obey the apostle Paul's command about marriage. Eventually, at the advanced age of twenty-one, I managed to quiet my qualms about authority, at least long enough to get through an engagement and wedding. I even said "obey" in the vows. But as for real-life submission to authority, my husband's or anyone else's, I've grappled with that ever since.

Twenty-four years later, however, middle-aged wisdom is finally making a dent in my independence. For one thing I've occasionally found myself in situations where what I needed, more than anything else, was someone with authority—and not my own. I remember one such incident last summer.

Our oldest, Sheri, had spent the summer working at Trail

Ridge Camp Cherith in Wisconsin. At the end of the summer I had to drive the four hours north to pick her up and make the annual transition from camp, to home, and back to college. I had been to the camp only once before, and even then I hadn't been driving, so my navigation technique leaned heavily on maps. Imagine my concern when I discovered that the local map, the one tracing the last fifteen miles of poorly marked tangled roads, was nowhere in the car. So, having already been scatter-headed enough to leave the map at home, I did the only remaining sensible thing. I drove to the nearest small town and began to make inquiries.

A corner gas station attended by a teenager turned up nothing. He'd never heard of the camp.

I tried a small shop down the street. "Yes," the elderly woman said. "I've heard of that camp. I know it's way out in the boonies." She sniffed at "boonies" and all those unenlightened enough to live so far from the civilizing influence of a Wisconsin small town. No, she didn't have a local map, and she wasn't sure which direction I should head into the boonies that encircled her civilized island.

I zig-zagged on to a general store, in search of a phone. But first I tried my question one more time. "Can you tell me how to get to Trail Ridge Camp Cherith?" The proprietor was as much help as the other people I'd interviewed. But a customer interrupted. Through a heavy speech impediment, she said, "Trail Ridge Camp Cherith? Hey, I've been there." I pulled out pencil and paper. A half hour later, I was hugging my daughter.

In that small Wisconsin town I was in no position to be my own authority. What I needed was someone who had "been there."

Jesus is such a person. So when religious leaders of His day questioned His authority, they got some thought-provoking answers.

Read aloud Mark 11:1–11.

1. a. How did people prepare for Christ's arrival in Jerusalem? _____

_____

_____

_____

_____

b. What notes of spontaneity do you see? _____

_____

_____

2. What aspects of Christ's arrival in Jerusalem would likely catch the attention of religious leaders? _____

_____

_____

Read aloud Mark 11:12–26.

3. a. What similarities can you see in Christ's treatment of the fig tree and His treatment of the temple? _____

_____

_____

_____

b. Why do you think Jesus treated the fig tree and the temple in such similar ways? _____

_____

_____

Note: Even though it was not the season for mature figs, the tree should have carried immature, green knobs of fruit, a frequent food for travelers and peasants.

4. a. Look again at verses 22–25. What three conditions does Jesus attach to answered prayer? _____

_____

_____

_____

b. What would you find difficult about praying in this way? _____

_____

_____

5. Why would Jesus' actions on this day further antagonize religious leaders? _____

_____

_____

_____

_____

_____

Read aloud Mark 11:27–12:12.

6. a. What do you think the religious leaders meant by the phrase "these things" when they asked Jesus the questions recorded in verse 28? _____

_____

_____

    b. Why were these important questions? _____

_____

_____

    c. How might the religious leaders have benefited if they had answered Christ's follow-up question correctly?

_____

7. What similarities do you see between the tenants in Christ's parable and the religious leaders who were questioning Him? _____

_____

_____

8. In what sense were these religious leaders also the builders referred to in verse 10? _____

_____

_____

9. Describe the different motives of the vineyard owner and his farmer tenants, citing particular actions that express these motives. _____

_____

_____

_____

10. What does this parable say will happen in the future of the people who heard it? _____

_____

_____

_____

_____

11. As you consider all of Christ's answer to the question of the religious leaders, what do you see included in the scope and source of His authority? (You may also look back at His actions discussed in the early part of today's study.)

_____

_____

_____

12. Why do you think the religious leaders were so resistant to Jesus? _____

_____

_____

13. When are you tempted to resist Christ's authority in your own life? _____

_____

_____

13

WHAT DOES JESUS DO WITH TOUGH QUESTIONS?

Mark 12:13–44

"A question is only as good as the answer it brings."

When I teach how to write inductive Bible studies, I sometimes open and close my teaching session with that statement. If people forget all that I've said in-between about personal study, outlining, lesson structure, group dynamics— and remember only that one statement, they won't go home empty-handed.

It's an opposite perspective from that of a college student who expressed fond memories of the family devotions led by his father.

"Dad would say, 'What do you think that verse means, son?' and I'd have to sit up and pay attention."

"What happened next?" I asked.

My friend seemed surprised that I thought much of anything would happen next. "Well," he stammered, "I said, 'I don't know.' Then Dad would tell us all what it meant."

This father was doing a great job in that he was leading his family in regular Bible study and prayer, a responsibility neglected by many Christian men. But he was underusing a magnificent tool: the question.

With only minor touching up, my friend's dad probably could have asked questions that would have had his children digging through the passage themselves and coming up with answers just as correct as Dad's. But the answers would be their own property: studied, hunted, and found by younger eyes.

Jesus was a master of the art of questioning. But He was also a master at giving answers. Mark 12 finds Jesus on the receiving end of hard questions—some of them with hostile intent. But He treats those questions with respect (no pat answers for complex questions). And when His questioners have finished, Jesus has a final question of His own.

Read aloud Mark 12:13–34.

1. Answer the three questions for each of the three sections.

a. Who asked Jesus a question? _____

_____

_____

_____

b. What was the question? _____

_____

_____

_____

c. What do you see as the motive behind the question?

_____

_____

_____

Look more closely at verses 13–17.

2. What differences do you see between the way these men addressed Jesus and the motive behind their question?

_____

_____

3. What do you admire in Christ's answer? _____

_____

_____

_____

4. What questions growing out of Christ's answer remain in your own mind? _____

_____

_____

_____

5. Why do you think Jesus did not give a more complete answer to this question? _____

_____

_____

Look more closely at verses 18–27.

6. What absurdities do you find in this question?

_____

_____

7. In verse 24, Jesus accuses the Sadducees of a twofold error. What had the Sadducees failed to understand in Scripture? How had they misunderstood God's power?

_____

_____

8. How is Christ's quotation from Exodus, "I am the God of Abraham, the God of Isaac, and the God of Jacob," an evidence for life after death? _____

_____

_____

Look again at verses 28–34.

9. What reasons did Jesus and this teacher of the law have to respect each other? _____

_____

_____

10. What is hard about obeying these commands?

_____

_____

_____

Read aloud Mark 12:35–44.

11. How could Jesus be David's Lord and also David's son? _____

_____

_____

_____

12. What contrasts do you see between the behavior of teachers of the law and Christ's definition of their most important laws? _____

_____

_____

_____

13. What additional contrasts do you see between the widow and the teachers of the law? _____

_____

_____

_____

14. a. Take one more look at what Jesus said were God's most important laws (vv. 30–31). What do you know about God that could help you love Him in this way? _____

_____

_____

b. How might obeying the first command help you keep the second? _____

_____

_____

15. What one thing could you do this week to bring you closer to keeping these two commands? _____

_____

_____

14

WHERE IS JESUS WHEN THE WORLD ENDS?

Mark 13

We lived in the country when I was a child. From our front yard I could view spectacular sunsets as they spread loftily over tassled Ohio cornfields. Sometimes the same view gave mountainous thunderheads—silver white on top and grayed by rain on the bottom. At other times I saw bright, hot blue sky faintly traced by cirrus mares' tails.

But my favorites were the keyhole clouds. I could look to the west and its boiling, tumbling mass. Then somewhere I'd see a keyhole patch of blue, perhaps edged by sunlit gold. *If I could peek through that keyhole*, I thought, *I'd find another world—one of harmony and light and beauty*. That cloud keyhole was just the setting I expected for Christ's return. Someday—maybe tomorrow or today or even right now— Jesus would burst right through that keyhole. And nothing would ever be the same.

As a child I viewed the prospect of Christ's return with a

mixture of feelings. Sometimes I didn't even want to look at that keyhole for fear of what I'd see there. And on an extra awful day, if I saw a keyhole in the clouds, I'd view it with two opposite feelings, neither of them admirable. One said, "Come on, Jesus, get me out of this mess." And the other said, "Don't come now; I wouldn't want You to catch me like this." But sometimes when my world was pretty much in order, I'd think, *Jesus, I know the preachers say we're supposed to be happy about You coming back, but couldn't You please wait? I've got a lot of living to do yet.*

I moved away from Ohio cornfields twenty-seven years ago. Even the house is gone. And I never saw Jesus step through the cloud keyhole. Not yet. But words from Scripture still set the stage. He said He would come. But when?

1. When you think of the end of the world, what do you see? _____

_____

_____

Read aloud Mark 13:1–4.

2. What reasons did the disciples have for asking these questions? _____

_____

_____

Note: This temple, clearly visible from the Mount of Olives, had been built by King Herod. Many of its stones were thirty feet in length.

Read aloud Mark 13:5–37.

3. What mixture of feelings do you think the disciples experienced as Jesus told them the information in this chapter? _____

_____

_____

4. What could the disciples know, from this talk, that might help them through Christ's coming death? _____

_____

_____

5. Like many prophecies Mark 13 blends two distinct events:

- The fall of Jerusalem and destruction of the temple in A.D. 70, which ended in the famous siege of Masada.

- Christ's second coming to earth.

Look through this chapter again and try to decide which of these two events each prediction best describes. (Don't worry if you aren't certain about some of them; Bible scholars aren't certain either.)

A.D. 70   **Christ's Return**

_____   _____

_____   _____

_____   _____

_____   _____

_____   _____

Look again at verses 5–13.

6. What hardships could Christ's followers expect to endure? _____

_____

_____

7. What dangers could come from thinking, as verse 7 states, that the end is closer than it really is? _____

_____

_____

Note: "He who stands firm to the end will be saved" (v. 13). The *New Bible Commentary* says, "To endure *to the end* probably means not to the end of the age, as in verse 7, but to the uttermost, as endurance which is complete" (p. 879).

Look again at verses 14–27.

8. What words and phrases show the degree of distress that people who live through these periods of time will see?

_____

_____

_____

_____

9. Even in these hard times, what indicates that God does not abandon His people? _____

_____

_____

10. a. Look again at verse 26. What mixture of emotions does this verse bring to you? Why do you feel this way?

_____

_____

b. How would you expect God's people, caught in the conditions described here, to feel about Christ's return?

_____

_____

Read again Mark 13:28–37.

11. Why did Christ tell His disciples about the signs of the end of the age and His second coming? Look for the clues in the parable of the fig tree and the parable of the man going away. _____

_____

_____

Note: The word "generation" (v. 30) has often caused a problem in interpretation. It may refer to the race of Jewish people, or it may refer to those present for the events of A.D. 70 (*New Bible Commentary*, p. 880).

12. a. Over and over in this chapter, Jesus tells His followers to "watch" and "be on guard." In view of the events written here but not yet fulfilled, how might you obey these two commands? (Be specific.) _____

_____

_____

_____

b. Why do you think Jesus did not tell His disciples when all this would occur? (See verse 32.) _____

_____

_____

13. Jesus said in the parable of the departing man that each waiting servant had his "assigned task" (v. 34). What do you see as a major task you are to do while you wait for Christ's return? _____

_____

_____

15

DOES JESUS KNOW ME BETTER THAN I DO?

Mark 14

How could anyone abuse a small child, I wondered as I sat in a meeting of foster parents and heard them describe the condition of children who came to their homes. Bruises, burns, broken bones, malnutrition seemed routine baggage for these stranded toddlers. *Their parents must be monsters,* I thought. *Surely no fully human beings with milk in their stomachs and blood in their veins could perform such violence.* I knew I could never do such a thing.

Months later God gave me opportunity to find out. My husband and I became foster parents. We took in five children in rapid succession. These added to our own two girls, who were five and seven years old. Some foster children stayed and some left, but for two years we had three toddlers, each bringing a unique set of demands into our home. We diapered, mopped, fed, bathed, and doctored at whirlwind pace. Eventually I fenced off the kitchen as my own "playpen" so that at least twice a day I could get some form of meal on the table.

One hot summer day the kids stood yanking at the toddler gate, yelling at top decibel as I tore around the kitchen trying to make supper. The potatoes boiled over, the phone rang, but I could barely hear it over the din. I raced toward the gate, a hand raised at an offending mouth.

In that moment I saw myself in a truer light than any amount of foster parent meetings had been able to manage. I too could abuse a child.

Peter, a three-year follower of Jesus, had a similarly skewed opinion of himself. But Jesus knew the real Peter and offered him an opportunity to prepare for his "moment of truth." I'm glad Jesus knows the real me too.

Read aloud Mark 14:1–31.

1. What different preparations for death do you see here?

_____

_____

_____

2. Why do you think Jesus did not criticize the woman for using such expensive perfume in the way she did?

_____

_____

Note: Nard or spikenard was ". . . imported from India in special, carefully-sealed alabaster jars, to conserve the perfume. It was only when some wealthy house owner received special guests that he would break the seal of the jar, so as to be able to do the anointing" (*The Zondervan Pictorial Encyclopedia of the Bible,* p. 502).

3. What do you think surprised the disciples as they celebrated Passover together? _____

_____

_____

4. Study more carefully verses 22–24, the first account of what we now call the Lord's Supper.

    a. What would the disciples find startling here?

_____

    b. What would give them hope? _____

_____

    c. Why would they want to re-enact this ceremony?

_____

5. Notice again Christ's prediction of betrayal and denial. As you study the disciples' response, what can you guess about their conflicting emotions? _____

_____

_____

6. a. What would constitute a serious threat to your own faith? _____

_____

_____

    b. If you were faced with that situation, what do you hope you would do to steady your faith? (Where would you go? Who would you talk to? What would you avoid? What would you read? What would you try to do or not do?)

_____

_____

_____

Read aloud Mark 14:32–72.

7. Suppose for a moment that Peter, James, and John had heeded the warning to watch and be on guard (Mark 13) and had prayed with Jesus in Gethsemane. What difference might this have made to Jesus? to the disciples? _____

_____

_____

_____

8. How did Christ's arrest and trial differ from what you would consider a fair procedure? _____

_____

_____

_____

Note: The young man who fled naked in the dark (vv. 51–52) was probably Mark, the writer of this gospel, a teenager at the time. Small wonder that he did not leave us his name.

9. a. Look more carefully at Christ's confession (vv. 61–62). If any listener had accepted that statement as true, what could that person have known about Jesus?

_____

_____

b. If such a person acted on these words, how would they affect the course of his or her life? _____

_____

_____

10. What pressures caused Peter to deny Jesus?

_____

_____

_____

11. Review each reference to Peter in this chapter.

   a. What do you admire in Peter? _____

_____

_____

   b. What differences do you see in the way Peter knew himself and the way Jesus knew him? _____

_____

_____

12. If you were to take a personal warning from Peter's experience, what would you caution yourself about?

_____

_____

16

WHY DID JESUS LIVE AND DIE?

Mark 15:1–16:8

Death causes us to take stock of life. Not long ago my husband's father died. He was eighty-five. During the last years of my father-in-law's life, his brain gradually deteriorated so that he traveled backward the steps of development he had taken as a child. For a while, in his mid-seventies, he seemed to work with the reliability of a twelve year old. Mom arranged for someone else to finish the remodeling job he'd contracted, and we encouraged him to sell his pickup truck. Mom stacked his business stationery in a box and put away her typewriter. Then one spring we noticed that Dad functioned more like a five year old. He followed Mom around the house with constant questions; we didn't dare leave him alone near the kitchen stove. But months later he was like a two year old. Speech was hard. Sometimes he fell. Eventually he needed to be lifted, rolled, fed. Finally even breathing was too hard. The backward journey was complete.

For Dad dying was a ten-year process. Yet his funeral was a celebration of life—not those last ten years—but the seventy-five before them and the life everlasting that he had entered. We talked about Dad's early years as a lumberjack in Swedish winters. We talked of the family Dad and Mom had created, one of the few families we know as yet untouched in any corner by divorce. We talked of Dad's eighth-grade Swedish education that he'd wielded to send every child to college. We talked about four children and thirteen grandchildren and a great-grandchild, all firm in the Christian faith. We talked about Dad walking the peaked roof of a house he was building, with a hundred pounds of two-by-fours on his shoulder while he sang at full voice, "Jesus Loves Me." And even while we cried, we celebrated together that Dad was now well and happy and complete with that Jesus who loved him.

Jesus' death brings about some of that same kind of reflection. For Him too death was long, not long in years but long in events. Each of the four Gospels devotes one quarter or more of the book to the last week of His life. For Jesus death was also long in significance, far more so than Dad's or any other human life. Like any encounter with death, reliving the death of Jesus brings grief. But it also brings opportunity to reflect on the impact of His life—and death—and life again.

Read aloud Mark 15:1–15.

1. This record is as much a trial of Pilate as it is a trial of Jesus. Based on the events recorded here, how would you judge Pilate? _____

_____

_____

Note: Pilate was the Roman government's administrator over Judea. Jewish religious leaders took Jesus to Pilate because, under Roman rule, Jewish people were not allowed to carry out the death penalty.

2. a. How did Christ's confession before Pilate differ from His confession before the religious leaders? (Compare Mark 14:61–62 with Mark 15:2.) _____

_____

b. In what sense was each confession true? _____

_____

c. Why was each confession dangerous in its own setting? _____

_____

Read aloud Mark 15:16–41.

3. Look again at Christ's prayer in Gethsemane (Mark 14:36). What different kind of suffering grew from Christ's words, "Not what I will, but what you will"? _____

_____

_____

_____

_____

4. What elements of truth do you see in the taunts recorded in verses 29–32? _____

_____

_____

_____

5. Review Mark 10:35–40. In view of the events of Mark 15, why do you think Jesus did not promise to give James and John what they asked? _____

_____

_____

6. a. Read Malachi 4:5–6, Mark 9:2–4, and Matthew 17:10–13. (The Malachi verses are the last two verses of the Old Testament.) In view of this background information, why might onlookers wonder about Elijah at the time of Christ's death? _____

_____

b. How would you have responded to their questions?

_____

_____

7. Look again at the centurion's statement (v. 39). What events surrounding Christ's death might convince an observer to become a Christian? _____

_____

_____

_____

Read aloud Mark 15:42–16:8.

8. Notice the role of women throughout this account. What seems special about their work and purpose?

_____

_____

9. What do you think went through Peter's mind when he learned of the angel's words recorded in verse 7?

_____

_____

_____

_____

Mark's gospel is incomplete. Though scholars have found several possible endings, the earliest manuscripts simply break off at verse 8. Perhaps an early scroll was torn and the fragment lost. But other writers help fill the gap. To find what happened when Peter obeyed the words recorded in verse 7 and went to Galilee, **read aloud John 21:15–19.**

10. What ingredients in this account would help Peter feel fully restored to useful service of Jesus? _____

_____

_____

At the end of Mark, Christ's followers are told to return to Galilee: "There you will see him, just as he told you." To understand the importance of these witnesses that Jesus was alive again, **read aloud 1 Corinthians 15:1–8.**

11. a. According to Paul, what are the major tenets of the Christian faith? _____

_____

_____

_____

b. How might a Christian, who was beginning to doubt that Jesus had risen from the dead, benefit from this section of Paul's letter? _____

_____

_____

12. How is your life different because Jesus lived and died and came back to life? _____

_____

_____

_____

13. Think about all you have learned during your study of Mark's gospel. What do you appreciate about Jesus?

_____

_____

_____

Pray to Jesus, thanking Him for these qualities in Himself.

HELPS FOR LEADERS

1 / HERE COMES JESUS!

Mark 1

Be sure to read the introductory chapters "I've Joined the Group. Now What?" and "Me, a Leader?" (pp. 7–14) as part of your preparation to lead this study. Point out these sections to your group when they get together. You should summarize the ground rules for them and ask that the group read these chapters carefully during the intervening week.

1. Use this question to involve each person in your group.

3. a. Your group should locate the following: Judea (v. 5), Jerusalem (v. 5), Jordan River (v. 5), Nazareth (v. 9), Galilee (v. 9), Sea of Galilee (v. 16), and Capernaum (v. 21).

b. Your group should point out these references to time: "At that time" (v. 9), "At once" (v. 12), "After" (v. 14), "the time has come" (v. 15), "near" (v. 15), "At once" (v. 18),

"Without delay" (v. 20), "When the Sabbath came" (v. 21), "just then" (v. 23), "As soon as" (v. 29), "That evening" (v. 32), "Very early" (v. 35), "immediately" (v. 42), and "at once" (v. 43).

c. If your time together is short, summarize the information asked in question 3a and b, and then discuss only part c.

4. Group members should point out all of John's actions in verses 4–9 noting how each of these fulfilled the prophecy (vv. 2–3) to prepare the way. Someone may also point out that even John's imprisonment (v. 14) made room for Jesus and His message.

5. Study verses 10–13. There is no need to struggle with weighty distinctions. Just encourage your group to comment briefly from the text.

7. Your group can answer this question from two different angles: 1) Why did Jesus choose *these* four men (John 1:35–42 will cast additional light)? or 2) Why did Jesus call disciples at all? Both questions are relevant.

8. a. See verses 28, 33, 37, 39, and 45.

10. Your group should point out the interweaving of these two forms of ministry. It is particularly apparent in verses 21–27 and verses 35–39.

11. a. For people skeptical about the supernatural, particularly the evil supernatural, Mark's frequent references to demons are likely to raise red flags. These people will wonder if the demons were a primitive way of describing mental illness, and they will wonder why Mark is so absorbed with accounts of demons. They may doubt the truthfulness of Mark's story.

The best tack for sailing through these murky waters is to let the gospel of Mark speak for itself. The leader can simply say, "Mark believed in demons. Mark says that Jesus believed in demons. But right now Janet doesn't believe in demons, and that's okay." Then continue to study what Mark says about them.

Follow-up questions to 11a include:
- What did Mark seem to believe about evil spirits?
- What seems to be the relationship between people and the evil spirits?
- How would you describe the relationship between Jesus and these evil spirits?

As for the frequent appearance of demons in Scripture, the *New Bible Commentary* says, "It is, however, a phenomenon especially associated with the period of our Lord's presence on earth. It is referred to only twice in the OT, and twice in the NT outside the Gospels, and it is clearly distinguished from mental disorders" (p. 856).

b. Compare verses 12–13 with 23–27, 32–34, and 39. For a fuller description of Christ's temptation, see Matthew 4:1–11 or Luke 4:1–12. Don't spend undue time on this question since the application sections of your study are still to come.

12. c. and d. Each group member who responds should address whichever of these two questions is most appropriate for her.

14. Questions 12 through 14 form a summary and application of this chapter. Save about twenty minutes to treat this section, then try to involve each person in some response.

2 / IS JESUS GOD?

Mark 2

1. Let this activity bring out the "ham" in your group. Enjoy this story from five different points of view, and in the process point up most of the information in the first twelve verses.

2. a. See verses 5–7. Alan Cole (*The Gospel According to St. Mark*) comments this way: "The teachers of the law saw at once down to the theological roots of the matter. Of course, none but God could forgive sin; how dare a man like Jesus claim such authority? Again and again during the life of Christ the same dilemma was to re-appear. If He were not divine, then He was indeed a blasphemer . . . ; there could be no third way out" (p. 66).

b. Several reasons appear in the text. That Jesus could draw crowds is graphically pictured here. Jesus could also read thoughts (v. 8). He claimed to forgive sins, a divine prerogative. And He gave visual proof that these sins were forgiven by healing the man.

If your group has not already discovered the information, ask a follow-up question: Why did Jesus heal the paralyzed man? (see v. 10).

4. A tax collector was even less popular in Christ's era than today. Then a tax collector was a Jew who acted as an agent of the foreign (Roman) occupying nation. Further, he gained his entire income by extracting from the people money beyond what Rome required. A house large enough to accommodate the dinner described here shows that Levi had been good at acquiring income. Yet Levi's occupation made him a social outcast and was a constant reminder of his own sinfulness. To follow Jesus, he needed only to give up his occupation. His need, he already recognized.

But the teachers of the law, perhaps because they were so religious, were not even this far along the path to receiving Jesus. They might have been able to keep their occupation, or some form of it, but to admit personal sin—when they had spent a whole life avoiding even touching a sinner—this was nearly impossible.

5. Notice how enthusiastically Levi shared with his own kind of people the opportunity to know Jesus. Notice also verse 17. Those who view themselves as spiritually healthy apart from Jesus will see no need to come to Him. It is only when we identify ourselves as we truly are (sinners) that we are ready to receive His healing and follow Him.

If your group is slow to see this, try a follow-up question: What did Jesus mean by comparing Himself with a doctor?

6. In this metaphor of the wedding Jesus is the bridegroom, and His followers are the guests. They do not fast, because they are celebrating His presence. But a time will come (Christ's death) when fasting and mourning will be appropriate.

7. The new wine represents Christ and His teachings. The Pharisees' strict adherence to the law (Old Testament law and Jewish tradition added to it) are like old wineskins. The new wine is too powerful to be contained in this old vessel. It will explode in all directions, as indeed it did throughout the Book of Acts. Yet Jesus invited the Pharisees to bring new wineskins to contain His wine. The unshrunk cloth and old garment of verse 21 illustrate the same incompatibility.

11. Paragraph divisions are vv. 1–12, vv. 13–17, vv. 18–22, and vv. 23–28.

3 / WHO IS CHRIST'S FAMILY?

Mark 3

1. Use this as an initial survey question. Don't expect detailed answers; they will come later in the study. Just help everyone contribute to an overview of the chapter.

2. Christ's question put the Pharisees in a difficult position. It was the kind of teaching question that would normally be used in a synagogue homily. The law said they could rescue an injured animal on the Sabbath; in fact it would be "doing evil" to let an injured animal die for lack of help. Was the man not worth more than an animal? In addition, tradition (Jerome) says that this man was a plasterer by trade; he needed both hands to earn a living. Interestingly, when Jesus asked whether it was better to "save life or to kill" on the Sabbath, the Pharisees responded by plotting to *kill* Jesus.

Yet the Sabbath laws were strict, and Jesus had just proclaimed Himself Lord of that Sabbath. If they acknowledged His right to heal on the Sabbath, must they also acknowledge His proclaimed position? And what would this do to their interpretation of Sabbath law? Not surprisingly the Pharisees kept silent.

Your group should think through some of these problems as they work with question 2b.

4. b. Your group should mention some of the following: Jesus used a boat. From it He could address a large group of people using the banked shore as a natural amphitheater. He could also get away if the press of the crowd became dangerous. Jesus also would not let the evil spirits announce His true identity. Eventually He withdrew with His close followers to the hills. He then selected twelve men to assist in carrying out His work.

5. Any number of reasons are possible. Perhaps Jesus did not want to speed up a fatal confrontation with Jewish religious leaders. Perhaps He wanted people to discover His true identity gradually on their own. Certainly He would not welcome "help" from an evil power, even a supernatural evil power. In any event people would not likely respond with godly faith to evil spirits.

Don't read answers like these to your group. Simply let them discuss the question until they arrive at most of these possibilities themselves.

6. a. Your group should notice the phrases, "Jesus . . . called," "they came," "He appointed." People may also remember previous encounters in Mark with five of these men: Simon (Peter) and Andrew (1:16–18), James and John (1:19–20), and Matthew (Levi) (2:13–17).

b. Three functions appear in verses 14–15. These men are to "be with him." He will "send them out to preach." And they are to have "authority to drive out demons."

7. Are there apostles today? Possibly not. But the three functions described here still go on, though authority over demons for most of us may translate into resisting evil in general or gaining victory over personal sin. Encourage your group to speak as specifically as possible.

8. See verses 21–22.

Did Jesus have biological brothers? This may prompt heated discussion in a group with a wide variety of churches represented. The *New Bible Commentary* (p. 860) responds in this way:

> On the subject of *his brothers* [verse 31] the literature is extensive, but three main views have been held. They were either Jesus' own brothers by blood; or half-brothers, the sons of Joseph by a former wife; or cousins, the sons of Mary the wife of Clopas and sister of the Virgin Mary. The second and third alternatives have been argued by some, principally Roman Catholic writers, in the interests of the dogma of the perpetual virginity of Mary. The available evidence is unfortunately not conclusive; but the fact that Jesus had His own brothers is the most natural inference from such passages as Mt. 1:25 and Lk. 2:7. From a doctrinal point of view it would, moreover, emphasize the reality and complete-ness of the incarnation.

9. If your group seems confused, try the follow-up question: "If Satan is the *strong man,* what is Jesus saying about Himself?"

10. For a more leading question, ask: What will happen to a person who continually mistakes the work of the Holy Spirit for the work of Satan?

Your group should come to conclusions similar to these: Jesus is warning the scribes that they have come near to serious sin. The Holy Spirit is God Himself. By attributing His works to Satan, the scribes were immunizing themselves to His witness. If the Holy Spirit, who draws a man or a woman to God, is persistently resisted, that person never can come to Christ. The sin of rejecting God is eternal. Many people fear that they have committed the unforgivable sin. The fact that they are concerned about this is evidence that they have not; God is still working in their lives. Your group, however, should come away from this passage knowing that God does not take blasphemy against His Holy Spirit lightly and that resisting the Holy Spirit has a dulling effect on future encounters.

11. Compare verses 20–21 with 31–35. For the end of the story, take a look at the constituents of the early church nucleus (Acts 1:14).

12. Your group should notice that in verse 23 Jesus *called* the teachers of the law to Himself and began to teach them. He explained the danger of their mistake in the strongest possible terms.

Note that He did not follow His family, who thought Him out of His mind and in need of rescue, home to Nazareth, but He continued the work His Father had sent Him to do. But He pointed the way for them to become members of His spiritual family as well as His biological family. Acts 1:14 shows that they accepted His invitation.

14. Save about ten minutes for these final questions of

application. Then encourage all who are willing to respond to them.

4 / WHAT HAPPENS WHEN PEOPLE HEAR ABOUT JESUS?

Mark 4:1–34

1. Try to get an answer from each participant. This will help everyone to feel a responsibility for making the study work. Be sure that they give verses for their findings. Repetitions that they may find are: parables, sow/sower, seed, listen/hear, kingdom of God, fruit/harvest, ground/soil, lamp/light.

2. In spite of Christ's interpretation of this parable, exact counterparts of the three main ingredients remain somewhat ambiguous. Let your group define them, as best it can, from the way they are used. They will probably come up with something like the following:

The sower is Jesus or anyone who spreads "the Word"— the message of Jesus or the teachings of Scripture.

The seed, Jesus says repeatedly, is "the word." But is this the word about Jesus, the message of the gospel of salvation, the teachings of Scripture in general, or some blending of all of these?

As for soil, it represents the many kinds of people who come in contact with "the word." Or is the soil the different ways they receive that word?

4. Jesus describes each type briefly in verses 15–20. Let your group elaborate on His description. What kind of soil were the Pharisees? What kind of soil were those who merely wanted healing? What kind of soil were His family? His disciples?

5. Some people may feel that this question is more confrontive than they'd like to answer, but a few should be willing to discuss it. If everyone seems hesitant, make some of these suggestions:

We should answer this question by looking at the effect of the Word of God on our lives.

- Do I easily forget it?
- Is my faith easily upset by argument or trouble?
- Do I follow God's Word for a bit, but then get interested in something else like a new house, new friends, or new activities?
- Do I hear and understand the Bible, make it part of my daily life, and willingly share it with others?

We can discipline ourselves to receive the Word of God and act on it. We can, if we want, become good soil.

6. Let your group wrestle with this question for a while. It doesn't have an easy answer, so expect disagreement. The question rises out of verses 11–12, 24–25, and 34. These are hard sayings, confusing to lay people and theologians alike. Here are several possible interpretations:

- Verse 12 merely shows the consequences of not acting on the message of Jesus. It does not show the purpose of the parables.
- Verse 12 is a deliberate exaggeration used to illustrate a point but not to be taken literally.
- Verse 12 is a judgment unbelieving people bring on themselves.
- Verse 12 shows that God has chosen to reveal Himself to some but not to others.
- Verse 12 provides protection against shallow acceptance of the gospel, the kind of easy belief followed by withering because the belief has no roots. A future immunity to Jesus' message might result. Therefore the parables kept people so they would not "turn and be

forgiven" *now,* but freed them for a more full acceptance of Jesus at a later time.

9. Verses 23–25 are sometimes mistakenly studied apart
from the parable they explain (vv. 21–22). The responsibility
of having heard and understood the gospel is stated here. To
increase our own faith, we must use it and share it (the
measure and the lamp stand). To remain silent will only
weaken our own beliefs. And to refuse to act may demonstrate that we never believed in the first place. This is not
hypocritical reinforcement, but simply God's method of
maturing His children and spreading His Word.

There is no need to read this explanation unless your group
is totally stumped. They will probably discuss their way to
similar conclusions because of their study of the previous
parable.

13. Encourage people to be as personal and specific as is
comfortable in the group. A single concrete plan of action
may spur several other people into work. If the conversation
tends to get too general, occasionally ask: Is this something
you think *you* should do?

5 / ARE MY NEEDS TOO BIG FOR JESUS?

Mark 4:35–5:43

2. Group members should remember first that Jesus had
just finished some strenuous teaching. Remember the four
parables of verses 1–34? Mark 4:1 describes the crowd as so
large that Jesus taught from a boat on the water's edge. Verse
36 suggests that He left "just as He was" in the same boat.
Even so the demands on Him were so great that other small
boats (v. 36) from the crowd accompanied Him. In addition

His sound sleep in an open boat under siege of storm speaks of exhaustion.

It's interesting to wonder how the storm and the subsequent calm affected the other small boats.

3. Possible answers include:

- If they were going to die, the disciples wanted Jesus to know that they were dying together.
- The disciples knew the storm was too strong for them to handle.
- The disciples needed His physical help in coping with the boat during the storm.
- The disciples were annoyed that Jesus was not experiencing their distress with them.
- The disciples hoped that Jesus would supernaturally quiet the storm.

4. a. See the details of verses 1–5.

b. See verses 15, 18, and 20.

5. The passage does not answer this question outright, so your group will likely disagree. At first, people may say that Jesus killed the pigs. But did He? Or did Satan (acting in petty vindictiveness through the demons) force the pigs into the sea? Or did the pigs simply kill themselves?

And why, if the demons soon were to suffer disembodiment anyway, did Jesus grant their request to enter the pigs? Was it to protect the man from harm when such a large number of demons were separated from him against their will? Or was it to make the pigs a visual demonstration to the man and the onlookers (with whom he would have to live) that the demons were in fact gone? Was Jesus saying to the demoniac and to the bystanders, "This man is worth more than two thousand pigs"? Or was the death of the pigs a simple statement from a Jewish teacher, "You have no business owning ceremonially unclean animals like pigs"?

Your group may discuss any or all of these possible

explanations. They probably will not reach a consensus. But the alternatives should keep them from assuming that Jesus was unnecessarily cruel to animals—or that He caused property damage without reason.

6. Your group should recall the initial condition of the man—so violent that people weighted him with heavy chains to try to slow him down. The group may also feel that the way the people treated this man is also an influence of Satan.

The conversation between Jesus and the demoniac, with the demons bargaining for bodies, illustrates Satan's work. People may notice that Jesus initiated help for the man. The reason the man was shouting and identifying Jesus correctly, as was usual for demons, was that Jesus was saying, "Come out of this man, you evil spirit."

But beyond the condition of the demoniac, your group can also see the work of Satan in subsequent events: the fear of the people and their asking Jesus to leave, thus cutting themselves off from His message of eternal life.

If you have extra time, you could discuss these related questions:

- What do these events reveal about the character of Satan?
- In what ways is this encounter with demon possession similar to others you have seen so far in Mark?
- If the Pharisees of Mark 3:22–30 had witnessed this scene, what would they have concluded?

8. a. Jesus would not remain where He was not wanted. Since His main purpose was to teach and to grant people eternal life through faith in Himself, a crowd hostile to Him as a person had already said no. Perhaps Satan's ugliest work here was not the ravages on the demoniac but his influence on the people to ask Jesus to leave—to their own eternal personal loss.

b. Jesus probably insisted that the healed man stay behind as a testimony to the townspeople of His power over Satan. They might believe that Jesus temporarily quieted the demoniac. Only as they saw the healed man day after day would they know Jesus' lasting power over evil. Verse 20 suggests that the healed man immediately began his work of witnessing to Jesus' power. He must have done his job well. By Mark 7:31–35, Jesus found a much more receptive crowd in Decapolis.

9. a. Your group should think of several answers:

● A synagogue ruler was more important than an outcast woman.

● Jairus's request was more urgent—his daughter was dying, while the woman already had lived twelve years with her problem. (It is interesting that those twelve years were the total span of the girl's life.)

● The two people's desire for attention differed markedly: Jairus pleaded publicly and earnestly; the woman wanted anonymity.

● Jairus had much more potential to influence other people to receive Jesus. The woman was a "nobody."

11. This is a good time to draw in people who are afraid of "hard questions." Here, all ideas are equally valid.

12. Find several details in verses 35–43.

13. Your group should arrive at titles similar to these:

Jesus is Lord over nature (4:35–41).

Jesus is Lord over demons (Satan, evil) (5:1–20).

Jesus is Lord over sickness (5:25–34).

Jesus is Lord over death (5:21–24, 36–43).

14. Allow as many as are willing to respond to this question, but don't probe past a comfortable level of privacy. If your group is able to pray, talk to Jesus together, bringing to

Him the needs that have been expressed. Encourage people to pray brief prayers for each other.

6 / WHEN IS BELIEF NOT BELIEF?

Mark 6

Today's study is unusually long. Begin promptly and pace the study with one eye on the clock. Be ready to summarize two or three questions, if necessary, in order to complete the study on time.

1. a. See verses 2, 6–7, 14, 31, 33–34, 44, and 54–56. Use these questions to get as many people as possible initiated into the discussion.

b. The problems of Christ's wide hearing appear throughout the chapter. In His hometown, people seemed to think He could not possibly be "for real." After all, He had come from them. Sending out the Twelve may have been good practice for the disciples. It also was a way of touching many people whom He could not reach because of the limits of a single human body. Once, when the Twelve returned to report, the persistent crowd demanded so much of their attention that the disciples didn't even have time to eat. When Jesus and the Twelve tried to escape by boat, the crowd followed on foot. By verses 45–46, we see Jesus holding them off while His disciples again leave by boat. Only then is He able to get time alone to pray. But by verses 55–56, we again see a press of sick people so intense that teaching seems impossible. So Jesus gives what they want. Even though their real need may have been for teaching, He heals them.

Let your group cover these points only briefly, since you will treat them in more detail later in the study.

2. It is comforting to know that some of the people mentioned later became leaders in the Christian church. James presided over the church in Jerusalem (Acts 15) and later wrote the book of James. Judas wrote the book of Jude.

4. a. See verses 12–13. Your group may want to compare the work described here with the original purpose of the Twelve, as described in Mark 3:14–15.

b. Note that Jesus sent them out in pairs and gave them authority over evil spirits. See also the details of verses 8–11. Your group ought to be able to link each part of the instructions with the ultimate purpose of the work. The gist of their findings will probably show that the disciples had to become dependent on the people they ministered to; they had to become dependent on the power and the message Jesus gave them; and they were not to waste time on an audience already determined not to hear. (Perhaps Jesus wanted to spare them rugged confrontations that demanded more mature faith.) The "two by two" standard would give them mutual physical and spiritual support.

7. Treat each character separately as your group examines the passage.

8. Did Herod commit the eternal sin described in Mark 3:28–29? Possibly. Herod listened enough to John to know some measure of the truth. Yet he refused to accept it. Now he felt guilty and worried, but not enough to request teaching from Jesus. Later, when Jesus stood on trial before Herod, Jesus did not say one word, even though Herod questioned Him. (See Luke 23:8–12.) Perhaps by then Herod had passed by all of the opportunities.

9. Death, of course, was an overriding threat. But encourage your group to look at other difficulties presented by this kind of ruler. His moral values would influence others to follow similar patterns. (This girl's dance was no light entertainment, if we can judge by the reward attached.) The possible persecution of new believers might discourage converts. Even Herod's feelings of guilt worked against Christ's purpose: Herod identified Jesus wrongly.

Encourage your group to explore these and other concerns.

10. The account about the death of John the Baptist forms an interlude between the disciples' missionary journey and their return. They needed to report to Jesus, rest, and eat.

11. Notice not only what Jesus did but also what He did not do. Normal human reaction to such a crowd, under these circumstances, would have been quite different.

12. Discuss the nature of Jesus and His relationship to those who follow Him.

Note: Several patterns begun here in Mark 6 were later picked up by the early church. Anointing sick people with oil (v. 13) was not the way Jesus healed, yet James 5:14 shows it a pattern of the church. Breaking bread (v. 41) later became part of the communion service, though here it was probably just a normal job of the host. "He gave thanks" (v. 41) is a pattern of saying grace before meals adopted by Christians all over the world. And how do missionaries go out? Usually two by two.

14. Theologians express diverse opinions about this question. Your group may come up with two of their major possibilities:

● When Jesus took five loaves and two fish and used them to feed five thousand men (plus women and children), He revealed Himself as the Creator God. A God who created a universe should have no trouble making a few thousand pounds of food. After all, He had fed a multitude manna for weeks in the wilderness (Exodus 16). The God who created all things, including the laws of nature, could walk on water if He chose. It was He who created the viscosity of water. And He could still a storm if He wanted. The winds and the rain were His creations.

● By feeding the five thousand, Jesus illustrated that He loved His followers and would care for them. Therefore they need not have been afraid of the storm or His sudden appearance on the surface of the lake.

"Was Jesus walking on a sandbar?" someone in your group may ask. Not likely, according to the text. Verse 47 places the boat "in the middle of the lake." And these fishermen who had based their income on knowing the lake's geography were "terrified" when they saw Him.

If you have extra time at this point in your study, try these additional questions:

● Verse 48 says that Jesus was about to pass His disciples by. Why do you think He stopped and got into the boat?

● What would be the advantages and disadvantages of the kind of reception Jesus got in Gennesaret?

15. Assign each section to different people in your group. Ask them to study silently for a moment, and then answer the questions in sequence.

16, 17. Save at least ten minutes to discuss these final two questions. Encourage as many as possible to participate. What is your own answer to question 17?

7 / AM I AS CLEAN AS I THINK I AM?

Mark 7

1. Let your group answer this question primarily from verses 1–5. This will show the surface area of conflict. Deeper issues will emerge as you study the entire passage in more detail.

2. Jesus spoke to the Pharisees and teachers of the law in verses 6–13, the crowd in general in verses 14–15, and His disciples in verses 17–23.

3. a. Corban was a custom whereby a person could set aside property or money as an offering to God. The person did not need to actually give the money at the time of his Corban vow; it could be passed on to the temple treasury after he died. This kept him from having to take care of his aging parents and let him use his money wholly for himself during his own life. Most of this information is given or implied in verses 10–13. Let your group discover this.

b. The Corban custom is an excellent example of Jewish disregard for the intent of the law while strictly adhering to its letter. It was a method to water it down to an acceptable but convenient law. Jesus sets their practice of Corban (where they broke a specific command of the Decalogue and thereby neglected their parents) against their scrupulous adherence to a mere tradition like ceremonial hand washing.

If questions 3a and b seem too elementary for your group, try this combined question: How did Jesus use the practice of Corban to illustrate hypocrisy?

4. a. See verses 14–15. The crowd would have had trouble comprehending something so opposed to the tradition they had been taught. In addition Jesus seemed to hint that impurity may be something over which they had little control.

b. See verses 14–23.

5. Draw from verses 14–23, especially the list of "evils" in verses 21–22.

6. a. If time permits, try this follow-up question: What practical steps could you take to teach these concepts to your own teenager?

7. Use this question to summarize all you have studied

thus far. A sharp-eyed participant may notice the frequent use of the word "tradition." It appears six times in these verses. If time permits, you could ask this question: Why are people likely to follow religious tradition rather than God's commands?

If your time for each study session is limited but the number of sessions you can meet is open-ended, consider breaking this study in half and ending with the optional question above.

8. The dialogue between Jesus and the Syrian Phoenician woman takes the form of a parable in which each person used symbols they both understood. If your group has trouble seeing the undercurrent of meaning, ask: Why (or what) were the children, the dogs, the bread, the crumbs? The group should then see that the children are the Jewish people; the dogs (little pets) are the Gentiles; the bread is the ministry of Jesus; and the crumbs are the leftovers (or second course) of His ministry. As in all of the early Christian work, the message is spread *first* (v. 27) to the Jews but later to all who will hear. The woman understood what Jesus was saying and claimed her proper position as second in line (though not necessarily second in importance) to receive the ministry of Jesus.

If your group has trouble arriving at these conclusions through discussion, try a second follow-up question: How might a correct identification of this woman's position before God help rather than hinder her belief?

9. This is a good opportunity to draw in people who may have grown silent during your discussion of more weighty issues.

10. Your group should make observations like the following:

- Jesus continued to demonstrate power over demons.
- Jesus showed that he could heal from a distance, the only recorded such incident in Mark.

● Jesus illustrated that His ministry was not only to Jews but also to Gentiles.

● Jesus continued to set an example of taking time for those in need, in spite of personal inconvenience.

11. a. Your group should note in verses 33−35 the various actions that would communicate to this man. Someone may also notice in verse 36 what a difficult command it was for a mute man who had been healed "not to tell anyone."

12. Notice the different reception of the people.

13. For places see Mark 6:53; 7:24; and 7:31. After leaving Gennesaret, the travels stayed mostly in Gentile territory. Not only were all foods clean, but, as Peter was to discover later in Acts 10, so were the people those foods symbolized.

If time is short, omit questions 12 and 13.

14. b. Jesus and the Pharisees held opposite views of humankind's original nature. The Pharisees said that we become "unclean" by touching the evil around us. Jesus said that we are "unclean" already because of what is inside us.

15. Save enough time for several people to express thoughtful replies to this question.

8 / WHAT DOES IT COST TO FOLLOW JESUS?

Mark 8

1. Try to involve each person with this question.

2. Mark 8:19−21 helps provide a summary of the first feeding. It also quotes Jesus Himself as referring to two separate miracles, thus challenging those who suggest that these are two tellings of the same event.

3. a. See verses 11−13.

b. Your group could discuss any number of possibilities in response to these questions.

The Pharisees wanted a sign "to test" Jesus. That alone may explain why He wouldn't give them one. They also wanted a sign "from heaven." Perhaps they considered the work He had done so far as earthly. Did they want voices and lights in the sky? Would they have believed them if they had experienced them? Besides, Jesus had been giving "signs" all along. These Pharisees could hardly have missed the miracles of healing and mass feeding, not to mention His inspired teachings. Perhaps Jesus knew there was no way these men would receive Him, so to their own great loss, "He left them."

4. a. The Pharisees, or teachers of the law, appeared in the following verses: Mark 2:16, 18, 23–24; 3:1–6, 20–29; 7:1–13; and 8:11–13.

b. Jesus asks at the end of this paragraph, "Do you still not understand?" And Bible students ever since have debated what it was the disciples were supposed to have understood. Let your group discuss their own ideas. They are likely as valid as anyone else's. Possibilities include:

- The "yeast" was the sin of saying, "Do it again—just for show." After all, the Pharisees had asked for a sign— which Jesus had refused to give—and now we see the disciples in a boat with only one loaf of bread just after collecting seven basketfuls, which we can presume they threw away.
- Or perhaps the "yeast" was the sin of mis-identity, attributing Christ's works to the works of Satan, as Mark 3:20–29 warns against. The identity of Jesus becomes a critical factor later in this chapter.
- Or maybe the "yeast" was simply a hardness of heart— a seeing but not seeing, a hearing but failing to

understand—a carelessness in perceiving the teachings of God.

● Was the "yeast" legalism, an attempt to obey the letter of the law but without turning all of one's being over to God? The Pharisees have thus far been most noted for their legalism, and Mark 7:9–13 criticizes their shallow commitment to the true cost of giving one's self to God. Once again the later part of this chapter (vv. 34–38) addresses that cost more fully.

Any of these interpretations, and perhaps many others, would find support in the text and provide possible answers to this question.

6. Relate verses 17–18 to verses 24–25. Jesus first healed the man's vision and then his perception—a much greater miracle. A man who had not seen for a long time would not understand what he saw, even though the eyes were healed. The brain too needed healing.

8. Not everyone will feel comfortable answering these questions, but wait long enough for two or three to respond. Be ready with an example from your own life. Even those who do not speak will benefit by hearing how others cope with these experiences and how God can reveal Himself in spite of them.

11. Use verses 31–38. There is no need to answer the second part of the question in great detail since you will treat it more fully in question 13.

12. Opinions will vary as you discuss this question. It will help to keep in mind Peter's character, and Christ's, as revealed thus far in Mark. It will also help to look at possible motives behind Peter's words as well as Jesus' words.

13. Encourage each person to phrase at least one question that grows out of these verses.

14, 15. Pace your study to allow ten minutes for thoughtful responses to these questions of personal faith.

9 / CAN JESUS HELP MY UNBELIEF?

Mark 9:1–32

1. Does Mark 9:1 belong with chapter 8 or chapter 9? Opinions vary. All depends, of course, on what Jesus meant by "the kingdom of God come with power." Here are some opinions:

- Jesus was referring to the transfiguration, described in verses 2–8.
- Jesus was referring to His death, resurrection, and ascension.
- He was referring to the destruction of Jerusalem in A.D. 70.
- He was referring to Pentecost (Acts 2:1–4).
- He was referring to the outreach of the kingdom of Christ to the Gentiles under Paul's ministry.

2. Any number of possibilities might come to mind. To Jewish thought, Moses represented the law, since God gave the law through Moses. And Elijah was the first of the prophets. So seeing each of these men talking with Jesus might have symbolized a link with fulfilling the law and the prophets.

The disciples also might have seen this as fulfilling the prophecy that before Messiah, Elijah would return. Or the disciples might have seen this as an exhibition of the "kingdom of God come with power," as Jesus had promised (v. 1). At the minimum the experience must have verified the disciples' faith in life after death. Elijah and Moses were long dead—yet the disciples saw them here alive.

3. See verse 5. Peter evidently assumed that what he saw in the altered appearance of Jesus and the presence of Elijah and Moses was a permanent state. He also may have recalled the tent of meeting (Exod. 40:34–35) where God's presence dwelt, and assumed that they should rebuild that kind of structure and perhaps the old relationships as well.

It is amusing to see that Peter "did not know what to say"—so he talked (vv. 5–6).

4. Draw answers from verses 9–13.

6. Somehow the disciples failed to comprehend that Jesus was going to literally die. (Why had they been so literal when He wanted them to think in symbols?) Therefore we see them discussing what Jesus could possibly mean by "rising from the dead" (v. 10). Then they asked the question about Elijah, who was to "restore all things," surely a welcome earthly kingdom in their minds. (Incidentally this statement shows that by now they assumed that Jesus was Messiah, else they would have had no reason to ask about Elijah.)

But, Jesus reminded them, John the Baptist died (recorded in Mark 6:14–29). Whatever restoration John was to perform was of a spiritual nature, not political. Just so, Jesus pointed His optimistic disciples to the prophecies not of a triumphant Messiah (that would come much later in another era) but of the suffering servant. This His disciples must face in their own immediate future.

7. This question will require some prior thought. You can help your discussion move more smoothly by reading it at the beginning of the session and asking people to be thinking about how they would answer it. If you prefer not to work that far ahead, allow a few moments of silence for people to collect their thoughts before expecting people to respond.

8. See verses 14, 18, and 28.

9. Demons are noted in the following passages of Mark: 1:23–27, 32–34, 39; 3:11–12, 14–15; 5:1–20; 6:12–13; and 7:24–30.

Is the description here an example of epilepsy? The *New Bible Commentary* replies, "Modern medical science would probably regard the case as one of epilepsy, but that is not incompatible with the view that the malady was caused by the presence of a demon with whom Christ directly deals" (p. 870).

Notice direct interaction between Christ and the demon in verses 20 and 25–26.

10. Your group should find several qualities or actions to admire.

11. See verses 5, 10, 19, 23–24, 28–29, and 32.

13. Use Mark 9:1–32, particularly the examples of unbelief you cited in question 11.

14. Not everyone will be able to address this question, but wait long enough for three or four to do so. People who are growing should find small instances in their past where, as they recognized unbelief (as Jesus forced the frantic father to do), God took that unbelief and by His own response to it turned it into faith.

15. If it seems appropriate after several people have shared a response to this question, close with brief sentence prayers, giving thanks for the growth expressed in question 14 and asking God's help for the needs people expressed in this question.

If all the people in your group are "pray-ers," just ask that the person sitting on the right of each person who shared bring that need or thanksgiving to God. If not everyone is comfortable praying aloud, suggest that those who are willing pray briefly. Or you can conduct a time of silent prayer with each person praying for the person on her right.

10 / WHAT MAKES A STRONG FAMILY?

Mark 9:33–10:16

With today's study, Jesus begins in earnest to teach His disciples. The study is unusually long, with an unusual number of opportunities for application. If your time together is too short to do it justice, consider breaking the study about midway (after question 7) and treating the second half in a separate session.

1. Answering this question could, if you let it, fill your whole time. Encourage fairly brief answers, but try to involve as many people as possible. Use it as a stepping-off point into the study, not as a substitute for it.

Be sensitive to anyone who grew up in a seriously damaged home. Be responsive to their expression of even a small strength, and don't ignore the hurt that such a past creates.

2. Be sure your group responds to both illustrations: the servant and the child.

3. b. Don't expect that everyone will feel uninhibited enough to respond to this part of the question. If two or three contribute, this will give the others examples to consider in their own relationships.

4. See verses 36–37.

11. See verses 5–8 and 11–12.

Moses' law about divorce appears in Deuteronomy 24:1–4. (It's interesting to note that by the law of Moses the woman was not free to divorce. Only her husband had that option. Christ, at least, put them on equal ground.) But even the law of Moses probably came as a protection to the woman. In divorce, according to Moses, the husband must give his former wife a written certificate. Then her status in the community could be certain; she was not merely deserted. And she could retain her dowry.

But Jesus pointed back to a law even older than Moses. Genesis 2:20–25, in telling the creation of woman, speaks these words so often used in wedding ceremonies.

Christ's teachings here will seem harsh to some, particularly to those who have suffered divorce. It is small wonder that in Matthew's account of the same event, the disciples exclaimed, "If this is the situation between a husband and wife, it is better not to marry." Try to create an atmosphere in your group that says, "Let's try to understand this passage together," not an atmosphere of accusation or judgment. God Himself will do the judging—and the forgiving.

15. See Mark 9:36–37, 42; and 10:8–9, 13–16. If time is short, omit or summarize this question. You should leave about fifteen minutes for the last two questions.

16. Don't expect everyone to answer each section—a couple of responses to each section is sufficient. But try to involve each member of the group at some point in this question.

11 / WILL JESUS TURN ME INTO A SERVANT?

Mark 10:17–52

1. Draw information from verses 17–22.

3. Discuss these questions as a single unit. Involve as many people as possible, but keep your eye on the clock.

4. The rich man came asking what he must *do* to inherit eternal life (v. 17). Instead of the answer the rich man wanted, Jesus told him what it would cost to follow Him (v. 21). Even the disciples who had followed Jesus for three years were shocked at the strict reply. "Who then can be saved?" they asked. *Can even we be saved?* they must have wondered. And Peter began to fish around for some semblance of obedience to Christ's standard in his own life.

Look for notes of hope and caution in verses 27–31. Discuss both sides. Notice the persecutions of verse 30, God's upside-down way of looking at people in verse 31.

Notice also verse 27, where it is God who does what is humanly impossible: an appropriate response to the young man's first question.

5. The disciples might have imagined anything. Some may have thought that Jesus was headed south to the religious and political capital of Jerusalem, where he would assume his rightful position of power. Others may have assumed that Jesus had an army waiting somewhere along the route—and it would take the practical steps necessary to give Jesus political control. Still others may have worried that persecution and death waited in Jerusalem.

6. Don't spend more time than necessary on this question. You should have more than half of your study time remaining.

7. On the surface we might assume that these ten disciples were angry simply because James and John had beaten them to the draw. They too would have liked those coveted positions next to Jesus in His glory.

But what did they mean by "glory"? It seems likely that all Twelve had totally missed the point of the preceding paragraph. They didn't see *baptism* and *cup* as suffering and death. Instead they expected an earthly political kingdom with Jesus as glorious ruler. And they all wanted a share in that glory.

It's possible, of course, that some of the ten did indeed understand Christ's meaning. If so, their indignation might express a righteous anger at the inappropriate nature of the request of James and John—in view of the fact that Jesus had just announced that He was about to die.

Did James and John actually hear Christ's predictions in the previous paragraph? Perhaps not. They may have already been deeply embroiled in their argument of who would sit highest in their imagined political kingdom.

Don't read the above ideas to your group. Much of it should emerge in any thorough discussion of the question.

8. Regardless of the reasons for the request and the indignation, Christ's teaching here speaks to the motives. Discuss these teachings in view of any of the separate motives that emerged in your previous question.

9. Linger long enough on this question to get a rather complete picture of this kind of leader. If your group has trouble working with the questions, try these follow-up questions:

● How can a Christian be a leader and a servant at the same time?

● If you were teaching a course in Christian leadership, how would it differ from a community-college course on how to get ahead in business?

10. Re-read verse 45 aloud, then let your group draw on all they have studied of Jesus thus far in Mark. If it seems appropriate (and if you have the time), the group may also draw on their general knowledge of Jesus. Just be sure they do not neglect the primary context of the statement: the Book of Mark.

12. Assign a quick re-reading of each of these four passages, then discuss the question together. Be sure to leave time to talk about the final question of application.

13. This question refers to the four passages in question 12.

Some group members may resent the idea that they should consider themselves better than their neighbors. Better or lesser character qualities are not the issue here. Instead we should see that Christ's teachings are indeed different from "standard operating procedure." If we are to follow them, we will behave differently from our neighbors—perhaps even from our own past actions.

Encourage most people to participate some way in this question.

Mark Littleton's poem "Bartimaeus" gives vivid witness of

this blind man's experience with Jesus. Practice reading it ahead of time so that you can close today's session with a good oral reading to your group.

12 / WHO GIVES JESUS AUTHORITY?

Mark 11:1–12:12

1. Preparations appear throughout these verses. They begin, of course, with Christ's deliberate trip from Galilee south to Jerusalem. Jesus timed His arrival to coincide with Passover, a time when religious leaders would congregate in their holy city. But Jesus too wanted to celebrate that holy day with His disciples in Jerusalem. Verse 2 finds Jesus sending two of His disciples ahead to borrow a colt. Had He made provision ahead of time with its owner? Or did He just *know* that the colt would be available? It's interesting that the colt had never been ridden. How did Jesus manage to control it in a noisy crowd? In any event the colt fulfilled the prophecy of Messiah in Zechariah 9:9—another preparation. Verse 6 shows that the people who witnessed two disciples taking the colt accepted the explanation. They too were prepared not to interfere. As for verse 11, here we see Jesus preparing for His actions of the next day.

For notes of spontaneity see especially verses 7–10. Yet even here we see a preparation from hundreds of years before. The people quote Psalm 118, a hymn traditionally sung at Passover, yet known to refer to the coming Christ.

Words from Psalm 118 frame today's study. You will see it again near the end, for Jesus Himself quotes from it in His final parley with the religious leaders (12:11). In view of their plans in 12:12, these leaders saw clearly Christ's claim.

2. Use this question to look at the events from the point of view of an established religious leader. You can also pick up any details missing from responses to the first questions.

3. a. Your group should notice that each received an initial inspection (vv. 11 and 13). Jesus took some verbal action on each: the curse of verse 14 and the explanation of verse 17. He also took forceful action to eliminate the problem (vv. 15–16 and 21).

b. Your group should notice the empty promise of each. The tree by its apparent life promised fruit—but there was none. The temple, also a thriving hive of activity, did not function for God's primary purpose: as a "house of prayer for all nations." Indeed the noisy buying and selling (and cheating) probably made prayer difficult. As for all nations, Jewish religious leaders had taken over as a temple marketplace what God had originally called "the court of the Gentiles."

If people are slow to discuss this question, try these questions:

- In what ways had both the fig tree and the temple ceased to function for the purposes God had designed them?
- Do you see Christ's actions with the tree and the temple as fits of temper or as righteous anger? Explain.

4. a. Your group should notice that we need to have faith in God (not faith in a specific answer to prayer but faith in God's character). Second, we must believe that what we ask will happen—and if we have met the first criteria of faith in God's character, we will make requests of Him that are in harmony with that character. Third, we must forgive—anything that we are holding against anyone.

Does our forgiveness from God hinge on our own ability to forgive? Yes and no. Many of the best manuscripts leave out verse 26 altogether. But of the problem, Alan Cole comments, ". . . unless we forgive our fellow men freely, it shows that we have no consciousness of the grace that we ourselves have received (Mt. xviii. 32, 33), and thus that we are expecting to be heard on our own merits. This would be a complete denial of the great principle of justification by faith; and so we cannot be heard. . . . We in our own unforgiving spirit have made it impossible for ourselves to accept the forgiveness freely offered by God since we refuse to adopt the only attitude in which it can be appropriated" (*The Gospel According to St. Mark,* pp. 181–182).

b. Draw in as many people as possible in discussing a response to this kind of prayer.

5. Review His actions of this day once again from the perspective of those already in charge of Jewish religion.

6. By "these things" the religious leaders probably meant all of the preceding events in this study: Christ's public entry into Jerusalem, His treatment of the fig tree, and His violent actions in the temple.

Of course the questions of verse 28 were important. If Jesus were acting on His own authority, He was insane. If He were acting on other human authority, He was a political threat and culpable of treason. But if He were acting on God's authority, then He was Messiah Himself. And if Jesus claimed that last source of authority, but religious leaders refused to accept Him, they could try Him for the most serious heresy.

Instead of falling into their trap of condemning Himself, Jesus asked His questioners a question. If they had given a serious and correct answer (that John's authority was from God), they would have had to take the next logical step: John was the prophet from God preparing the way for the long-promised Messiah, and Jesus (also with authority from God) was that Messiah. Had they taken that step, these religious leaders could have benefited from Christ's final teaching and could have led their people to true faith.

7. See verses 2–7. Compare these with the planned action of the religious leaders in verse 12. Though it's not stated, these same religious leaders had probably contributed to the death of John the Baptist (Mark 6:14–29).

Move through questions 7 and 8 rather quickly so that you can give more time to question 9.

8. Verse 10 quotes Psalm 118:22–23, another section of the Passover psalm previously quoted by the excited crowd in Mark 11:9–10.

9. Discuss the motives of both the vineyard owner and the farmer tenants. Verses 1–2 show the owner giving protective care of the vineyard. And verses 2–5 show patient persistence in trying to bring in the harvest. Verse 6 shows the owner's sacrificial love for his vineyard. He sent the son, *whom he loved.*

Yet the tenants were equally persistent. That their motives were selfish and that they knew the identity of the son is evident from verse 7.

Did the religious leaders know the same when they asked Jesus the question of Mark 11:28 and when they made the plans of Mark 12:12?

If your group has not yet correctly interpreted the parable, point out that each character in the parable fits Christ's current scene. Then ask them to identify each. They should discover that the vineyard is the Jewish people; the tenant farmers are the religious leaders; the owner is God; the servants are the prophets (including John the Baptist); and Jesus is the son.

10. See verses 7–11. Your group should note the following:

● The religious leaders will kill Jesus (v. 8).
● God will punish the religious leaders (v. 9).

● The position (of being God's chosen people) that Jewish people then enjoyed will go to others (v. 9, see also Mark 11:17).

● Jesus will be rejected by His own people (v. 10).

● Jesus will also be exalted as the capstone or crowning glory of the new faith.

11. Use this question to briefly summarize all of today's study, but leave at least ten minutes for the last two questions.

12. Encourage most people in your group to participate in some way in the final two questions. Expect both honorable and dishonorable reasons for resistance to Jesus.

13. Encourage people in your group to speak specifically enough to strengthen them in particular situations of future temptations.

13 / WHAT DOES JESUS DO WITH TOUGH QUESTIONS?

Mark 12:13–44

1. Examine each section separately, addressing all three questions for each section. Then move on to the next section. Divide the passage in this way: vv. 13–17, vv. 18–27, and vv. 28–34. Treat these questions briefly since you will study each section in detail later.

3. Jesus faced a lethal combination in the alliance between the Pharisees and Herodians. The Pharisees were key religious leaders. They were custodians of the religious law, responsible to protect it and keep it pure. The Herodians were Jewish political leaders who had sided with Herod, the ruler appointed by Rome to keep order in the Jewish land it occupied.

As might be expected, Pharisees and Herodians were natural enemies to each other, yet they joined to try to catch Jesus in this religious/political question. If Jesus said, "Pay taxes," He would anger Jews who resented and resisted Roman rule. But if He said, "Do not pay taxes," He could be tried for treason.

4. Take time for several to express their remaining questions about this difficult area of loyalty to state and loyalty to God.

Was Jesus simply cagey, walking a tightrope between two opposite forces who could kill Him? Or was He maintaining the natural ambiguity of overlapping and divided loyalty? We owe allegience to both God and the state. And in a conflict we must decide our position on the merit of individual circumstances. See Romans 13:1–7 and Acts 5:29 for related teachings.

6. Your group should notice, among other absurdities, that the Sadducees (who did not believe in a resurrection) asked a question that assumed resurrection. In addition the multiple deaths and serial marriages seem unlikely.

Note: The law of Moses that these Sadducees cited is the law of levirate (Deut. 25:5–10), a law designed to protect a woman's property rights and posterity. A man would marry, with her consent, his brother's widow. Any children born to this new marriage inherited his brother's property and carried on his brother's name.

7. See verses 24–27. Notice that here and in the following section, Jesus quoted only from the first five book of the Old Testament—the only part of the Scripture accepted by the Sadducees. Jesus reasoned with them from their own frame of reference.

8. Notice that when God spoke to Moses, He did not say, "I *was* the God Abraham. . . ." Even though these men were dead, God spoke of having a current relationship with them, as if they were still alive.

9. See verses 28–34 for each person's reaction to the other.

Once again Jesus quoted from the Pentateuch, the first five books of the Bible, when He responded to this question. The first quotation is the Shema from Deuteronomy 6:4–5. Devout Jewish men recited the Shema twice a day and wore its printed script in their phylacteries as part of their clothing (*New Bible Commentary,* p. 877).

Jesus added to the Shema (a command about God) a second command, a command about people. It appears in Leviticus 19:18.

10. Encourage as many as possible to discuss this question.

11. If people are slow to see this connection, ask: Who was holding conversation in Psalm 110, where David writes, "The Lord said to my Lord"? These words appear to be a conversation between God the Father (the Lord) and His Son (my Lord). So Jesus was "my Lord" to David during David's lifetime. Yet Jesus descended from David through His adopted father, Joseph (see Luke 2:4).

12. Your group should pick out six aspects of religious behavior in verses 38–40. Compare these with Christ's standards in verses 30–31.

13. Compare verses 41–44 with verses 38–40.

14, 15. Leave at least ten minutes for these questions. Encourage all who are willing to respond to them.

14 / WHERE IS JESUS WHEN THE WORLD ENDS?

Mark 13

1. Involve as many people with as wide a variety of answers as possible.

2. The questions here are the last of the long series of questions that began at Mark 11:28. Several factors, however, recorded in Mark 13:1–3 lead to these two particular questions.

3. Don't attempt to analyze the chapter in detail yet. But help your group express the variety of emotions the disciples must have experienced as Jesus revealed each new coming event.

4. Encourage group members to point out several strengthening aspects of this prophecy. For example, the disciples now knew that severe stress lay ahead; they could brace for it (vv. 9–13). They could also know that the Holy Spirit would help them in times of arrest (v. 11). They could know that Christ's words—all of them—would never fail (v. 31). They could also know that Jesus would return "with great power and glory" (v. 26).

Note on verse 11: Jesus promised special help from the Holy Spirit. But believers should not use this passage as an excuse for sloppy sermon (or teaching) preparation. Public speakers may feel that they are on trial, but their congregations are hardly a match for the setting described here.

5. Allow enough time to cover the major events of this chapter. Expect some disagreement. One expert suggests that verses 5–12 and 24–27 refer to Christ's return, while verses 2, 14–23, and 28–31 refer to A.D. 70. But opinions vary. The point is that Jesus predicted both events, that He gave certain warning signs for each, and that He expected His followers to be prepared for both.

6. Notice the worldwide hardships (vv. 7–8) as well as those directed specifically against believers (vv. 5–6 and 9–13).

7. Your group should think of several reasons for this warning. Followers of Jesus might identify the wrong person as the returned Christ. They might think the worst is over when it is yet to come. They might let down their guard against false teaching. They might stop working for God too soon.

8. Use this question to outline the host of hardships in this passage. Try to involve each person in your group.

9. Notice Christ's invitation to pray (v. 18). In verse 20, we see that God shortens these days for the sake of the "elect" or "chosen." (Even unbelievers benefit by the presence of these chosen people.) When verse 22 speaks of false Christs who attempt to deceive the elect, the passage admits that these false prophets are doomed to failure, at least with the protected people. (Notice the small phrase, "If that were possible.") Then there is the ultimate rescue (vv. 26–27), again directed to "the elect."

10. a. Don't expect everyone to respond with acceptance to this announcement of Christ's return. Novices to Bible study may be hearing of it for the first time. And even long-time believers who are honest with themselves will likely view this event with a mixture of feelings. You should expect your group to speak of such emotions as disbelief, shock, puzzlement, fear, apprehension, joy, relief, thanksgiving, and hope—to name a few. As each person names a feeling she associates with these verses, ask her to elaborate a little on why she feels this way.

b. If your group doesn't notice, point out the kind of entry to the scene described in verses 26–27. This might affect the feelings of those present at the time.

12, 13. As with all questions of application, the best way to answer is to begin with the word "I." Encourage as many people as possible to respond in some way.

15 / DOES JESUS KNOW ME BETTER THAN I DO?

Mark 14

1. Try to involve each person in your group with this question. Each person should see the preparation of the chief priests and teachers of the law (vv. 1–2), the preparation of the woman from Bethany (vv. 3–8) and Jesus preparing her onlookers at the same time, the preparation of Judas (vv. 10–11). Jesus continued to prepare His disciples in verses 17–21, 22–25, and 27–28. Peter understood Christ's warning of verse 27 and volunteered his own form of preparation in verse 29. And verse 31 sees the others following suit.

2. The tone of the passage suggests that this was a special occasion, a preparation of Jesus and His followers for death.

If we are tempted to use this example as an excuse for our own self-indulgence, the passage has enough evidence to give us pause. First, Jesus' followers seemed to assume a responsibility for the poor, as verse 5 states, and Jesus says nothing to negate that responsibility. On the contrary, His phrase "The poor you will always have with you" sets a deliberate contrast to His own imminent death. Jesus quickly followed His statement by the reminder, "You can help them any time you want."

Group members should point out details from verses 13–16, 18, 22, 24, 27–28, and 30.

4. Outsiders often accused early Christians of cannibalism. Christ's words about body and blood must have startled even those closest to Him. Apart from them, Christ's clear meaning that the time of His death was at hand (v. 25) must have added to their consternation. Yet the same verse offers hope to them—and to us. A day will come when Jesus Himself will eat bread and drink wine with us.

Encourage as many as are willing to speak of reasons why

followers of Jesus will want to re-enact this ceremony performed regularly, to this day, in most Christian churches. Someone may recall the added command in Luke's account, "Do this in remembrance of me" (Luke 22:19).

5. See verses 17–21 and 27–31.

7. None of us can be certain what difference this change would have made. Perhaps Jesus would have found comfort in His friends. Perhaps His friends would have been slower to turn tail and run. Perhaps Peter could have stood up to the accusations of the slave girl. But perhaps, with human weakness what it is, everyone would have behaved in much the same way anyway—with only an added sense of belonging to each other.

Let members of your group explore several possibilities together, at least forming a link with the previous study and the immediate pressure in today's account.

9. Beliefs, if they are sincere, will translate into action. While the believer may not consciously say, "Because I believe that I will see Jesus coming on the clouds of heaven, I can cheerfully wash my dishes today with a sense of purpose," under the surface the belief points to the act. In Christ's era a belief of this magnitude would make dramatic changes in action. Let your group explore these.

Someone may point out the similar claims recorded in Mark 14:61–62 and Mark 13:26–27.

10. The setting leading up to verses 66–72 created pressure. Yet, in Peter's defense, we must admit that he at least followed Jesus this far. Verse 50 shows that the others had deserted Him and fled long ago. Still, when pressed, Peter uttered three denials, each under increasing pressure and each with increasing vehemence.

Encourage your group to look through the details of verses 66–72 in search of these pressures.

11. See verses 27–31, 33, 37–38, 47, and 54–72. (John

confirms that verse 47 speaks of Peter, and Luke records that Jesus healed the wounded ear.) Don't forget to note Peter's reaction to the whole sequence in the last words of the chapter.

12. Encourage several different kinds of responses from as many group members as are willing to speak of personal reaction.

16 / WHY DID JESUS LIVE AND DIE?

Mark 15:1–16:8

2. a. Translations vary in recording Christ's response to Pilate, so be prepared for some discrepancies. The intent of the confession remains much the same.

c. In the religious setting, Jesus confessed that He was the Christ (Messiah). If it were not true, He was guilty of blasphemy. In the political setting, Jesus seemed to admit that He was "King of the Jews." While this statement was true in a spiritual sense—and in fact meant the same thing as His previous confession—in a political setting it sounded like treason. Blasphemy and treason each merited death by execution.

3. Use this question to help your group focus on the details of Christ's death. You can try this follow-up question: In what ways did Christ's death lack dignity?

4. There is an element of truth in each taunt, making them all the more cutting.

"Destroy the temple and build it in three days." Jesus would indeed perform this act. But the temple He had spoken of was His own body (see John 2:19–21). And He was at that moment making good His promise.

"Come down from the cross." Jesus could have exerted His divine power and simply walked away. He had already chided Peter about the misuse of force when Peter cut off a servant's ear at the time of Christ's arrest (Matt. 26:52–54). The twelve legions of angels He spoke of then were still available. Yet Jesus chose to remain on the cross. Was it harder because He could leave, than if He had no choice?

"He saves others . . . but he can't save himself!" Only Jesus knew that these two goals were mutually exclusive. Only because He was at that moment giving Himself to save others, could He not save Himself.

"King of Israel." Jesus was indeed the spiritual King of the Jews. He was their long-promised Messiah. And He was executed for that "crime." The sign above His cross could not have been more accurate.

Linger on this question long enough for your group to discover the truths and the irony in these taunts. If you need a follow-up question, try: Why were these taunts particularly cruel?

5. Many reasons could come to mind, so encourage your group to express some of these. Among them, James and John simply did not know what they were asking for. Their view of "glory" had nothing to do with a cross. So instead of James and John two robbers shared the spots they craved. (Yet, as John 23:39–43 records, one of these robbers became a believer.) In addition the early church would need James and John as witnesses of Jesus, His works and teachings. And in the end they too would drink a cup of suffering for the cause of Christ (see Acts 12:1–2 and Rev. 1:9).

If your time is limited, you should omit this question in order to allow enough time for the final questions of response to Mark's gospel.

6. b. See verses 34–36.

7. Try to involve each person with this question that

summarizes the events surrounding Christ's death. Since each person at the crucifixion (and in your group) brings a different frame of reference, answers should vary considerably.

If no one points out the torn temple veil and its significance (v. 38), do so yourself. The Jewish high priest alone could go through that veil, and he only went once a year. At that time, his purpose was to make atonement before God for the sins of the people. So the torn veil is a wealth of symbolism.

8. Use all of today's passage, but don't spend too much time here. A major portion of the study remains. If time is short, you may summarize answers to this question or omit it altogether.

10. Your group should point out several events that led to a sense of restoration.

11. a. Your group should find four points in verses 3–5. Paul stresses their importance in verse 2 by saying, "By this gospel you are saved."

b. Notice the variety of people who witnessed Jesus alive after His death (vv. 5–8). Paul also challanged the Corinthians to verify his statements by indicating that most of the witnesses were "still living."

Perhaps one of the greatest evidences for Christ's resurrection is that the people who were there believed it. They had not expected Jesus to come back to life. They had everything to lose by propagating such a tale. Yet they staked their lives on it. No wonder they took reassurance from its many witnesses. As Paul points out later in this chapter, the whole Christian faith rises or falls on this central doctrine.

12. Try to save ten or fifteen minutes for these final two questions. As part of the response to this question, someone should point out the concepts behind the words "saved" and "sin," used in 1 Corinthians 15:1–3.

13. After several people have responded to this question, suggest a brief time of worship prayers to Jesus. You can encourage many people to participate in a concise way by leading with a simple one-sentence prayer yourself.

BIBLIOGRAPHY

Aharoni, Yohanon, and Michael Avi-Yonah. *The Macmillan Bible Atlas*. New York: The Macmillan Company, 1977.

Archer, Gleason L. *Encyclopedia of Biblical Difficulties*. Grand Rapids: Zondervan Publishing House, 1982.

Cole, Alan. *The Gospel According to St. Mark*. Grand Rapids: Wm. B. Eerdmans Publishing Company, 1961.

Douglas, J. D., ed. *The New Bible Dictionary*. Grand Rapids: Wm. B. Eerdmans Publishing Company, 1962.

Guthrie, D., J. A. Motyer, A. M. Stibbs, and D. J. Wiseman. *New Bible Commentary*. Rev. ed. Grand Rapids: Wm. B. Eerdmans Publishing Company, 1970.

Roberts, David. *Yesterday in the Holy Land*. Trans. Ed van der Maas. Grand Rapids: Zondervan Publishing House, 1982.

Tenney, Merrill C., gen. ed. *The Zondervan Pictorial Encyclopedia of the Bible*. Grand Rapids: Zondervan Publishing House, 1975.

Vine, W. E. *An Expository Dictionary of New Testament Words*. Old Tappan: Fleming H. Revell Company, 1966.